THE TROPOHOLIC'S GUIDE TO INTERNAL ROMANCE TROPES

CINDY DEES

CYNTHIA DEES PUBLISHING INC

To my hundreds of students over the years, who taught me most of what I know about writing, thank you for your endless curiosity and pushing me to always keep learning.

INTRODUCTION

Go ahead. Groan. Everyone does when they hear the word trope.

In recent decades, the word trope has come to stand for clichéd, trite, boring, predictable plots and plot devices. Writers have been encouraged to layer trope upon trope, overusing and abusing them until they've become a bad joke in the publishing industry and a thing to be assiduously avoided in the screenwriting industry.

Authors, editors, producers, readers, and viewers alike have turned their noses up at tropes, unfairly maligning them without understanding them at all. But in reality, tropes are absolutely fundamental to the writing process and form the foundation of all stories. That's right. *All* stories.

They're big. They're powerful. They're archetypal. They're the stuff of myth and legend. They shape all the great epic love stories and give structure to all your favorite plots on the page and on the screen. In fact, they form the core of every great story ever told.

It's time to bring tropes out of the ridiculed corner and restore them to their proper and prominent place as essential tools for all writers. I plan to do this by:

-- properly defining what tropes are
-- showing how they're the vital building blocks of all storytelling

-- demonstrating why they're the key to creating unforgettable stories that resonate

powerfully with readers and viewers

You might want to read that last bullet point again. I'll wait for you.

First, a note about how this and the subsequent books in this series are organized.

When I first set out to make a list of all, or almost all, of the classic tropes used in romance novels of *any* romance sub-genre, my initial list came out at well over a hundred of what I started calling universal romance tropes—meaning each trope is applicable to every genre of romance and any type of love story.

To be clear, you don't have to be writing a romance novel or a romantic screenplay for these tropes to be useful to you. If you're writing a story of *any* genre that also happens to contain a love story, or even just a romantic relationship, read on.

When I started writing detailed analyses of each trope, it quickly became obvious that a single volume containing every universal romance trope would come out to well over a thousand pages. Hence, I launched into the daunting exercise of trying to figure out how to divide them into some sort of logical groupings.

After many failed experiments, I finally hit upon a way to divide tropes into four categories that made sense in the context of how they get used by writers.

I will be the first to admit that these divisions are somewhat arbitrary. It could easily be argued that any of the tropes might fit one or more of the other categories. However, I will show you in a later exercise how to choose one trope from each of the four categories I've established to create a complex, layered, multi-dimensional story.

That said, here are the four categories of universal romance tropes I came up with:

INTERNAL TROPES – These are the tropes of personal affliction: the wounds, fears, and personality traits that form obstacles to love inside the hearts and minds of your story's hero and heroine.

EXTERNAL TROPES – These are comprised of people, situations, and problems around your hero and heroine that prevent them from blissfully and naturally falling in love and finding their happily ever after.

BACKSTORY TROPES –As the name implies, these tropes are made up of the lingering problems, scars, and needs from your hero's and heroine's pasts that must be overcome before they can achieve happiness and true love.

HOOK TROPES – These tropes might more accurately be called Inciting Incident Tropes. They're the trope-based way your hero and heroine meet and come together as a couple and how that initial meeting establishes a set of problems that must be overcome before the hero and heroine can achieve their happily ever after.

All of the universal romance tropes resonate through the history of storytelling and continue to adapt to any time, place, or format. They work in novels, comics, TV, film, video games—you name it. They can be found in any genre or sub-genre of fiction, regardless of whether the tale is comic or tragic, a suspenseful thriller, taut murder mystery, science fiction adventure, or madcap farce. They adapt readily to any situation in which two people fall in love over the course of a story.

Story is story is story. Any story with a romantic element is a candidate for using one or more romance tropes to give it structure and movement.

They are truly the universal tropes of love.

In this series of universal romance tropes, I am confining myself to the tropes that apply to **any** type of fiction in **any** format. If you're writing an epic fantasy novel, a hardboiled crime thriller, a giant MMO video game, or the next Oscar-nominated family saga screenplay, and you have a romantic relationship in your project, these tropes apply to you.

These universal romance tropes also apply to **any** genre of romance. Meaning, it doesn't matter whether you're writing historical romance or alien-abduction romance, inspirational romance, romantic suspense, or romantic comedy. All of the tropes I've identified as universal are applicable to pretty much all romance genres and sub-genres.

Each of these trope types is no more or no less important, valuable, or powerful as a foundation for your story than another. They all are the stuff of classic romance story structure.

HELPFUL HINT: In this book, the two main love interests in each trope are referred to by the terms "hero" and "heroine" purely as a device for telling apart the main protagonists. Gender identity is interchangeable and exchangeable in every example, and not limited to just two people.

HOW TROPE WRITE-UPS ARE ORGANIZED

The table of contents lists in alphabetical order every trope included in this volume of the universal romance trope series. An appendix at the back of this book includes a list of all 141 universal romance tropes I've analyzed and which volume they appear in.

As for the write-up on each trope, it's probably easier to show you how it's broken down than it is to describe it to you. Below, I've randomly chosen the FORBIDDEN LOVE trope as a sample of this book's organization. My annotations for each section of the trope's entry are added in bold text for ease of identification.

Feel free to skim over the write-up itself. It's merely included here to give you an idea of how the rest of this book is organized and how granular the detail is on each trope.

And yes, EACH write-up on EACH trope in this series of books on universal romance tropes runs from six to eight pages in length. This is meant to be an encyclopedic reference providing complete information on each trope—gathered in one place for you.

I've developed this book as a handy guide for working writers. It's meant to streamline your plotting and planning, speed up your drafting, keep you from getting stuck or unstick you when you do stall mid-story, ensure your revisions catch all the big plot holes and pitfalls, and help you aim your story squarely at your audience in a way that will be deeply satisfying to your readers or viewers.

FORBIDDEN LOVE

We'll talk more about what tropes are titled in a bit, but I've tried to choose the most common names in use today that are also the most self-explanatory and easily recognizable to you.

DEFINITION

This is where I break down the trope in detail, analyze it in depth, and discuss any variations on the trope that are common.

DEFINITION of Forbidden Love

This is a trope of two people who are, for some reason, forbidden to love each other. There may be an excellent or deeply entrenched reason why they're not supposed to be together, or it can be an altogether specious reason. Regardless, the act of ignoring this prohibition is fraught with danger and will exact a very high price upon the lovers if they are caught...which they inevitably will be in your story.

This story typically features distraught lovers, a great deal of drama, sneaking around, fear of getting caught, and angst galore. These people know they shouldn't love each other or be together, and yet they simply can't stop themselves. Their passion is too great to resist or even restrain.

It's also possible the lovers see some compelling reason why they should be together. They may think the reason they're forbidden from being together is stupid, ridiculous, outdated, or in need of reversal, and in this case, they may defiantly pursue their love and unconsciously—or consciously—hope to get caught. They may want to flaunt the rules and openly challenge them.

Either type of couple—the worried, secretive one or the openly defiantly one—is in for a rough road when they do finally get caught. They have their work cut out for them not coming to a tragic end.

At its core, this is a trope of rebellion and the price of that rebellion. The culture, system, or rules against which the hero and heroine are rebelling will set the tone for your story and its level of darkness, danger, fear, or its level of farce, silliness, and humor.

Unlike the Across the Tracks/Wrong Side of the Tracks or a Cross Cultural/Interracial/Interethnic tropes, in which the lovers *may* face strong disapproval, anger, and pushback, in the Forbidden Love trope, the lovers *will* face serious and inevitable legal consequences, punishment, or even death for disobeying a hard and fast rule, law, or taboo (along with the disapproval, disappointment, anger, and pushback of family and friends).

ADJACENT TROPES

If this particular trope is close to what you want to write, but not quite right, you might want to check out the trope write-ups for one or more of these similar, but not exactly the same, tropes I've collected for you here.

Also, if you're looking for further inspiration or more things to think about while working with this trope (in this case, Forbidden Love), you can check out these similar tropes and find additional elements to add to your characters and plot.

ADJACENT TROPES of Forbidden Love
--Following Your Heart

--Feuding Families
--Rebellious Hero/Heroine
--Dangerous Secret
--Across the Tracks/Wrong Side of the Tracks
--Cross-Cultural/Interracial/Interethnic Romance

WHY READERS/VIEWERS LOVE THIS TROPE

This is a deceptively useful little list. It's worth thinking seriously about the kind of experience you want to give your reader or viewer. This list will give you some starting insights as to why your audience is drawn to this particular story arc. This list will also give you some idea of what kind of experience you need to deliver to your readers or viewers if they're going to fall in love with your project.

This list is not meant to be exhaustive by any means. It's merely a jumping off point for you to consider what your audience wants from this trope and if you're delivering that experience.

WHY READERS/VIEWERS LOVE FORBIDDEN LOVE

--it's typically a highly charged trope that takes the audience on a roller coaster
emotional journey
--we love to root for the underdog who's up against impossible odds
--your partner loves you enough to risk his/her *life* to be with you
--your partner will *die* for you

--we all like to think we would be heroic enough to defend our deepest values

and/or true love with our lives

OBLIGATORY SCENES

As the title suggests, each trope has a traditional starting point, it develops in a predictable way, it reaches a crisis in a certain way, and it resolves predictably. This is where we explore in detail the archetypal requirements of telling this story in a satisfying way to your audience.

Keep in mind, your audience already KNOWS how every classic story trope should go. Deviate from some version of these obligatory scenes at your own risk...

OBLIGATORY SCENES of Forbidden Love

THE BEGINNING:

The hero and heroine are introduced to the audience, possibly separately or just before their paths cross. They may need to start the story apart while the writer establishes the forbidden-ness of any potential relationship between these two people. In this scenario, when the hero and heroine do meet, they know up front that any relationship between them is a very, very bad idea. Hence, their decision to pursue a relationship is probably driven by overwhelming attraction and informed by a shared sense of understood risk.

OR

The hero and heroine may meet without understanding who the other person is or that a relationship between them would be a terrible idea. They may enter into the early stages of a relationship before they find out who the other person is and how forbidden continuing with the relationship would be. In this scenario, they have a terrible choice to make right away—a choice they will have to make again and again as the story progresses—of whether to continue on with the relationship or call it quits before they get caught.

The consequences of getting caught may be spelled out right up front such that the audience is fully aware of the risk, or these consequences may only be hinted at, creating a sense of questioning and suspense in your audience. Of course, it's possible the hero and heroine don't yet know the full consequences of their actions, in which case the audience may not find out right away, either.

The early stages of the relationship may happen completely in secret, or the couple may enlist the aid of a few trusted confidantes. These confidantes will undoubtedly advise strongly against continuing the relationship and serve to heighten the tension and sense of risk. If you choose to add confidantes as accomplices to your story, the stakes are raised as the hero and heroine put other peoples' lives in danger, too.

Remember that, at its core, this is a trope of rebellion and the consequences of that rebellion...on steroids. The beginning typically introduces the system, rules, situation, or person(s) the lovers will spending most of the story rebelling against. The sky-high stakes these lovers are flirting with are almost always established early in the story for your audience, as well.

THE MIDDLE:

The hero and heroine begin to fall in love. Much of the action of the story revolves around arranging and pulling off their trysts, and on scenes with the hero and heroine in their separate worlds, living a lie where they pretend not to be in love with the forbidden person.

If the consequences of the hero and heroine getting caught

haven't been made clear before now, they definitely will be spelled out in the middle of the story.

The middle typically includes desperately romantic stolen moments, near misses with getting caught, and a rising sense of desperation in the hero and heroine the more they fall in love with each other.

It's not uncommon for lovers of this type to fall in love fast and for the relationship to move quickly. They probably have very limited time together for the relationship to develop, so each scene in which they're together is likely a significant scene with substance and that moves the relationship forward. There won't be many or any scenes where they just hang out together casually. Every moment is stolen, and every moment counts for these two.

The middle is characterized by increasing emotion, increasing stakes, and increasing risk. As the lovers continue to get away with spending time together, they may be emboldened to go for something bigger—consummating the relationship, eloping, getting married in secret, or the like. This bigger goal they try to pull off is often the one that will ultimately lead to a crisis and disaster.

BLACK MOMENT:

The lovers are caught. All is lost. They are pulled apart and the consequences of their ill-advised romance lands upon them (and possibly on anyone around them who helped them). Their gamble hasn't paid off. Not only have they lost their relationship, but they may now lose the person they love and face terrible repercussions themselves.

A black moment in this trope is bad. Really bad. As a writer, do not hold back on letting fly with all the terrible consequences you've promised earlier in the story. The devastation should be complete as you rake your characters and your audience over the coals.

. . .

THE END:

The hero and heroine are rescued, redeemed, or forgiven in the happy version of this trope. The lovers find a way to convince the authorities around them, those responsible for enforcing the rules, norms, customs, or taboos they've broken, to forgive them. The lovers snatch victory from the jaws of terrible defeat and are allowed to be together, after all. They may be forced to leave their home and go into exile, or they may flee to a place where they're safe or where nobody knows them.

Even though they end up together, in this trope they usually pay a great price before the story is over. It can be a price paid as punishment for their transgression, or a price levied upon them in return for their freedom. Often it is both.

Remember: this couple did break the rules. Depending on what that rule is, your audience may be angry if the lovers don't pay a price of some kind for their rebellion or infraction. If it was an unjust rule, your audience may cheer if the lovers find a way not only to escape but also to avoid retribution or punishment for their transgression.

KEY SCENES

Of course, it takes more than four major scenes to fill a novel, take up an entire movie, etc. Most tropes suggest other important events or moments between your main characters as their relationship and the story unfold in a way unique to this particular story arc.

The additional scenes in this list are not mandatory in the same way the obligatory scenes are. These are just a few typical scenes you might choose to include in your story as you flesh out the plot. They're meant to help you brainstorm and suggest things to consider doing next if you get stuck.

. . .

KEY SCENES of Forbidden Love

--the moment when the hero and heroine realize that their love is forbidden

--the moment when the real penalties for getting caught are made clear to the lovers

and to the audience

--the moment when the hero and heroine (maybe together or maybe individually)

have a crisis of doubt about their decision to pursue this forbidden relationship

--the moment when a friend, family member, or other supporter finds out about the

forbidden and secret relationship and that person's reaction

--the hero and heroine's last moment together before they're torn apart forever

--the hero and heroine's moment of reunion at the end

THINGS TO THINK ABOUT WHEN WRITING THIS TROPE

This section is a detailed list of questions to guide your plot/character development and prompt thought about many of the major decisions you will need to make before you tackle writing your story or you'll want to ponder as you're discovering your way forward through your story.

Many writers tell me they come back to this list when they get stuck in the middle of drafting their project. Often, browsing through a bunch of questions like this can provoke a new idea or story direction. If you're REALLY stuck, you may also want to browse through the Things To Think About When Writing This Trope for one or more of the adjacent tropes listed earlier in this trope write-up.

You can also use this list as an editing/revision checklist. Have you included the major decisions and developments these questions cover, or are there areas in your story that need fleshing out, beefing up, or further explanation?

THINGS TO THINK ABOUT WHEN WRITING FORBIDDEN LOVE

How do the hero and heroine meet? It is an accident or chance? Do they recognize each other immediately, or do they have no idea who the other one is?

Do the hero and heroine know a relationship between them is forbidden when they meet, or do they not learn that until later? If later, when and how?

Why is this relationship forbidden? Do the hero and heroine think this is a good, reasonable, or just reason *before* they meet each other? If so, how do they feel about the restriction on being in a relationship *after* they've met? Is it still a good rule?

Who enforces this prohibition on a relationship between the hero and heroine? Is this person the villain in your story? Is this person reasonable and right to enforce the prohibition? Does more or less everyone around this authority figure agree with the rule that makes the relationship forbidden? Are they right to agree or not?

What are the consequences to the lovers of being caught together in a relationship?

Who around them finds out about their relationship but keeps it secret or aids and abets the relationship? Why does this person help?

What will the consequences be to anyone who helps the lovers be together? Are the consequences less or the same as those faced by the lovers?

Who sends a warning shot across the bow to the hero and heroine that there will be bad consequences for anyone who breaks the rule(s) that the lovers are secretly flouting? How is this warning sent?

How will the hero and heroine sneak away for stolen moments and trysts together? They may use different tactics every time they meet, or they may repeat the same tactic.

How does each tryst get slightly more dangerous than the last one? What causes the stakes to go up each time?

Do the hero and heroine meet in a situation where they have to pretend not to know each other or to be in love with each other? How does that go? Does anyone around them pick up on something...off... between the lovers or get suspicious?

How far will they take their relationship in secret? Will they sleep together? Get married? Get pregnant?

What are they trying to do when they finally get caught? Is it just another tryst, or is this tryst special in some way?

How do the lovers get caught? Are they betrayed? Is it accidental? Do they make a mistake?

Who separates them, and how are they kept apart?

Are the full consequences promised earlier in the book leveled at the hero and heroine or not? If not, why not?

Are the consequences for the hero and heroine the same or different? Are they punished by the same person or by completely different people? For example, do their own individual families, clans, kingdoms, or governments punish them separately under different sets of rules? Or does the same official or person in authority punish them both under the same set of rules?

Does the hero or heroine own up to having done a bad thing by breaking the rules? Are they defiant about having broken the rules? Do they try to bargain with whoever's going to enforce their punishment?

Will the hero and heroine finish suffering the consequences before they get back together, or will they be pardoned, escape, or in some other way evade the full measure of the consequences? If they avoid some or all of their punishment, how do they do this? Do they do it together, or individually in separate pardons or escapes?

If the hero and heroine escape punishment, this may be the most difficult part of the story to pull off plausibly. Systems of control and punishment are typically designed to prevent escapes and are very hard to break free of. Also, your hero and heroine are probably separated, so two different escapes must be coordinated and timed simultaneously.

Where will they go after they're reunited? Can they stay home or will they have to leave? If they must leave, where do they go?

Are they known where they go or not?

What happens to their friends who helped them be together in secret? Are these people okay at the end of the story? How will the hero and heroine ensure these people are okay, assuming they're still alive?

TROPE TRAPS

While I make no claim to have thought of every trap you can fall into with any given trope, I've done my best to capture as many landmines lurking within each trope as I can. This is where they're listed.

This list is also useful to read through and use as a thought exercise as you plan your story. I'm told by many writers that they find it, too, to be a source of ideas and inspirations as they plot, draft, or get unstuck.

TROPE TRAPS of Forbidden Love

Creating a hero and/or heroine who is more in love with the idea of love than their actual partner. Meaning, one or both of the characters gets so caught up in the tragic romance of it all that they lose sight of the very real risk and of the person they're actually in a relationship with.

Creating a couple that doesn't seem plausible for the long run. It may be all drama and danger now, but when all of that is gone, these two people are going to drive each other to distraction in a bad way and never survive as a couple for a happily ever after.

Creating a TSTL (too stupid to live) villain who enforces the rules even if they're silly or stupid rules.

Bonus trope trap: Failing to have the rule(s) the lovers are breaking make sense to the person(s) enforcing them. (although it's okay for the rules not necessarily to make sense to the lovers or your audience).

Not creating serious enough consequences for getting caught to sustain all the drama and secrecy the hero and heroine engage in. It's not enough for the hero and heroine to think the consequences would be horrible—the reader or viewer has to believe it, too.

Creating implausible situations where the hero and heroine get away with stealing a moment together but in which the audience knows they would normally be caught and should have been caught.

The lovers using the same tactics to be together over and over—when someone with an ounce of common sense around them would have caught on long ago to the tactic and caught them.

Not creating near enough misses with the lovers getting caught, which is to say, failing to keep your audience on the edge of its seats.

Creating a lame scenario in which the lovers are caught.

The lovers themselves create a lame or overcomplicated plan to be together that goes awry.

Failing to follow through on the consequences that were promised to the lovers and the audience at the beginning of the story.

Relying on a lame save to pull the hero and heroine out of the proverbial fire so they can be together at the end of the story.

Relying on an abrupt about face or change of heart in the person meting out punishment to relent and let the lovers be together out of the (brand new and heretofore unseen) goodness of his or her heart.

I can't tell you how many of my Asian friends loved the movie, Crazy Rich Asians right up to the moment where the dragon mother sees her son unhappy, has a change of heart, and gives him her engagement ring so he can go get the girl. That's when my friends universally groaned and said something to the effect of, "No Asian dragon mother would ever back down after having successfully chased off the woman she doesn't like or approve of for her son!" While I'm sure that's not universally the case, don't create a villain who suddenly acts completely out of character for no good reason to let the lovers be together in the end.

FORBIDDEN LOVERS TROPE IN ACTION

Last but not least, these are lists of movies, in some cases television shows, and books that use this particular trope. If you're looking for further inspiration for your story or want to see what this particular trope looks like in action, I've gone ahead and collected examples for you here.

Movies:

- Romeo and Juliet (the personification of the tragic version of this trope)
- The Thornbirds
- Dirty Dancing
- Titanic
- Guess Who's Coming to Dinner?
- Pride and Prejudice
- Clueless

Books:

- Birthday Girl by Penelope Douglas
- Twisted Games by Ana Huang
- Slammed by Colleen Hoover
- Matched by Allie Condy
- Daughter of Smoke & Bone by Laini Taylor
- Vampire Academy by Richelle Mead
- Delirium by Lauren Oliver
- The Sweetest Oblivion by Danielle Lori
- Red, White & Royal Blue by Casey McQuiston

2

WHAT ARE TROPES AND WHY DO THEY MATTER?

The term *trope* gets bandied about frequently in the publishing world and screenwriting world. Editors and producers watch carefully which tropes are selling well and chase those trends. Marketers and publicity departments aggressively signal tropes in back cover copy, trailers, and advertising posters. Artists faithfully convey tropes on book covers—cue the cowboy, cute baby, or Greek typhoon. Even online fiction retailers sort fiction by trope, although they typically call it category or keyword. Moviemakers follow their structure faithfully while filming and go out of their way to signal which tropes they've used even in movie titles.

Why do these tropes matter, you ask?

Because **the vast majority of readers choose their reading material largely based on the tropes inside stories, and the vast majority of TV and film viewers choose their content based on the tropes inside the shows and movies**.

Sure, readers fall in love with the work of individual authors and become devoted fans. Likewise, TV/film viewers fall in love with the work of a specific screenwriter or director.

But this is probably because most authors, screenwriters, and directors tend to return to the same tropes (or related and similar tropes) over and over in their creative projects. I propose that one reason why readers and viewers become super fans of individual story creators is, in part, because they all share an affinity for a similar set of tropes.

Authors and screenwriters explore and write about what they know, what they're comfortable with, or what's fascinating to them. Like readers and viewers, most story creators have favorite tropes they go back to again and again in telling their stories.

This tendency to repeat tropes is an important source of consistency in reading/viewing experience and, in fact, largely defines that writer's brand.

Let me repeat that. **Your brand is defined by the tropes you write over and over again**.

You can try like the dickens to brand yourself as a Sally Sunshine rom-com writer and put all the cute, cartoon covers you'd like on your books or movie posters. But if the stories you deliver to the reader/viewer are the tortured journeys of lonely vampires, cowboys, and gothic recluses, no amount of marketing is going to change the type of story readers and viewers associate with your name.

So, let me state what I said above in a slightly different way. **The stories you write over and over ARE your brand**.

I hear some of you out there saying, "But I write all over the map. I might do a cute secretary-boss rom com, then a dark, tortured historical set piece with a wounded hero, then a western-themed opposites attract story, and as a palate cleanser I might play around with a bit of alien menage-à-trois."

Congratulations! You're a really versatile writer! However...you have a branding problem. How will any reader or viewer see your name attached to a project and immediately know what to expect from the story you want them to buy or watch? Keep in mind the purpose of branding is to help readers and viewers find, as easily as humanly possible, a book, TV show, or film (or play, comic, graphic novel, video game, or song lyric) that they'll love and tell all their friends about.

We could spend a chapter or two of this book debating whether or not a great cover and title are enough to fully brand a book or if a great title and great trailer are enough to fully brand a TV show or film, but I stand by my statement that your NAME will be closely identified with the repeating tropes in the stories you create.

It's also likely that, as you develop a decent-sized backlist over time, you will start to see tropes repeating themselves in your projects no matter how many genres or sub-genres of fiction you write in, no matter how varied the screenplays you write.

All human beings have tropes that personally resonate with them and hold particular importance in our psyches and lives. We all tend to read and write those tropes, not to the exclusion of all others, of course, but with the most frequently.

We are drawn to reflecting on the things that have caused us plea-sure or pain, trauma or healing, and we all tend to spend years chewing on and examining those life events, themes, and lessons that have had the most significance in our own lives.

There are a bunch terrific books on the market about self-branding (I highly recommend Your A Game: Winning Promo for Genre Fiction by Damon Suede and Heidi Cullinan) if you'd like to explore the subject more.

At any rate, the important takeaway is that **the majority of readers and viewers return to the same tropes over and over in their reading and viewing preferences**.

A second key takeaway is that **it might behoove you to consider how this tendency in readers or viewers will affect your branding, sales, and audience loyalty**.

This idea is so important that we should probably dive into it a little deeper. In Lisa Cron's seminal work, Wired for Story, she compellingly argues that mankind survives and thrives because of stories, so much so that our brains are literally hard-wired to crave them. We live vicariously and learn through reading, watching, or hearing about the fictional or real experiences of others, and we're literally drawn to stories as a survival instinct.

In his book <u>Hit Makers</u>, a study of what makes some stories, songs, movies, fashions, or fads mega-popular, Derek Thompson presents overwhelming evidence that the stories people are most drawn to—in whatever form they happen to be told—have a strong element of familiarity with just enough newness to it to keep it interesting.

Thompson cites study after study proving that people gravitate to stories they're familiar with. They don't want to work too hard to have a good idea of where a story is going, and they actually prefer to have a good idea of how a story is going to end.

Indeed, in one study, some people were given spoilers of books, including descriptions of their endings before they read the books while others in the study read the same books without any advance knowledge of them. Consistently, the people who knew in advance how the story would end, and even what the big twists in the stories would be, rated the books *higher* in enjoyability.

Why does this matter to us as writers? Because tropes are predictable. They have a predictable beginning, middle, and end. And consumers of stories *like* this. In fact, they *crave* this predictability.

I hear some of you howling that readers and viewers get bored of consuming the same story over and over. You're not wrong—readers and viewers want enough surprises and twists to keep a story from being completely predictable. But they are comforted by and happier reading or watching a story that doesn't make them work *too* hard to follow it. Thompson calls this *fluency*. Readers and viewers want to feel smart and grasp the general bones of a story without having to hurt their brains to figure out where it's going.

I propose that one of the most powerfully familiar elements in any story is its trope(s). It is the trope that defines the shape of the story and reliably predicts for the reader where this story is going to go.

We all grow up absorbing and memorizing tropes whether we're aware of it or not. Everywhere we look we see tropes in action—from cartoons we watched as little kids, to literature taught in schools, to our entertainment—be it television, movies, video games, comic books, music lyrics, or some other format of story.

If I were to ask anyone, anywhere, at pretty much any time in human history, to tell me a story about two people who've grown up together as friends and then suddenly realize they're more than friends, I would get told a story that follows the classic friends-to-lovers trope **every single time**. If I specified that it should be a love story, the friends would overcome their reservations about the changing nature of their relationship and end up happily ever after, every single time.

Some stories are so universal they follow the same pattern every time they're told. The lessons we learn from these classically patterned stories are relatively the same every time, as well. And yet, we go back to them over and over and over.

They're familiar. They resonate with us at a deep, visceral level. We want to see them come out the same way every time. In fact, we *need* them to come out the same way every time as a means of reassuring us that the world we live in is predictable and safe.

These universal story patterns *that we all know already* are tropes. I'm merely naming, writing down, clarifying, and expanding on classic patterns of storytelling that have existed pretty much since the first stories were ever told by mankind. Obviously, new variations on ancient tropes get added over time and as societies evolve, but the cores of all classic tropes remain pretty much unchanged.

It's worth pointing out that, in the same way readers and viewers tend to be drawn to certain tropes that have special significance in or applicability to their lives, most readers, viewers, and writers also avoid certain tropes like the plague.

Perhaps a trope reminds a reader or viewer of something painful in their own past, or perhaps they personally disagree with the premise of a certain trope. Or maybe, they just don't like a particular kind of story.

Whatever the reason for their dislike of a particular trope, a viewer will change the TV channel or walk out of a movie in the middle, and a reader will put a book down—or throw it against a wall —and never finish it if they discover they've accidentally started consuming a story with a trope they despise.

And heaven help the writer who doesn't deliver on the promise of the trope(s) they've set up in a story or promised in its marketing materials. Readers and viewers are *outraged*—

Wait, let me shout that. Readers and viewers are OUTRAGED —when tropes aren't followed through on...but we'll come back to that in a minute.

PRO TIP: You have to pick your battles in the publishing and TV/film businesses. But fight, and fight for all you're worth, with your editor, producer, and marketing department to make sure your title, cover, blurb, back cover copy, trailer, posters, marketing materials, and advertising do not mislead readers or viewers into expecting a different trope than you deliver in your story. If you're self-publishing or inde- pendently producing your work, make this an absolute priority as you choose the packaging, marketing mate- rials, and sales strategies for your work.

I wrote a novel that a publisher tried to title, <u>Diving Deep</u>, and wanted to put a male Navy SEAL on the cover of the book in diving gear about to plunge off a boat into water. Deep sea treasure or ocean rescue adventure by a hunky soldier, right?

Nope. The book focuses on a woman trying to prove she's good enough to become a SEAL, and she spends the entire book in a land-locked, arid, mountainous region struggling to keep up with her SEAL instructor and rescue a kidnapped friend. She never even comes near water and neither she nor her boss ever puts on scuba gear.

How furious would readers have been if they bought this book expecting an underwater adventure focusing on a hot guy along with oceans, danger at sea, maybe sunken treasure, and they got my story instead?

Not to mention, how many sales would I have lost from readers who like a good kidnapping-and-rescue tale or a story of a spunky woman proving her worth to her boss, but who had no idea my story was about those?

Bottom line: Get the packaging, marketing, and advertising right when it comes to letting readers and viewers know what tropes will be in your story.

As an aside, this is why no story you ever create will ever be all things to all people. There is no such thing as a story that appeals to everyone. There are always bound to be readers or viewers who despise the tropes you've used in your story. But luckily, there are also bound to be readers and viewers who love them.

All you can do is faithfully tell the story dictated by the trope or tropes you chose to write about and hope that like-minded readers or viewers who particularly enjoy that trope or trope combination will find your story and love it.

This is also why there is no such thing as a marketing campaign or ad that will make everyone who sees it go buy your book or go watch your movie. All you can do is accurately signal to potential audience members what tropes are in your story and hope people who love that trope will give your work a try.

It's fine for potential consumers not to click through to your story or choose not to watch it. In fact, you want some readers or viewers—those who despise the tropes you wrote about—to stay far, far away from your story and never, ever write a scathing review of your work!

Your tribe of readers, viewers, or other story consumers is out there. For every trope or combination of tropes you can imagine to write about, there are plenty of like-minded people who have a special affinity for exactly those tropes and who crave stories built around that story structure.

EXERCISE: FINDING THE TROPES YOU LOVE

In order to find out which tropes you are most drawn to and tend to return to over and over, let's do a brainstorming exercise.

1. Take a few minutes to write down as many of your favorite things as you can think of.
2. Because this is a writing exercise, be sure also to think about things that make your favorite stories your favorites. What do you absolutely adore about them? You can draw from books, movies, video games, chitchat among friends, or any other way you consume stories.
3. If you've written stories before, you can include the tropes from those stories that you particularly enjoyed writing in your list.
4. Also, if you've noticed repeating trends in the stories you prefer to read, or the television/films you prefer to watch, you may have already started identifying the tropes that are totally your jam (and the ones you won't go near with a ten-foot pole). Add the tropes you know you love to your list.
5. Because tropes do not always have happy endings, now add to your list negative events or themes that tend to recur over and over in your life or in the stories you consume. I was

shocked years ago when a reader pointed out to me, some thirty books into my career, that I tended to write absent or disengaged fathers over and over again in my work. And yes, my own father was both of those things. Go figure.

6. Don't forget to include settings you like, types of characters that really excite, delight, or fascinate you, favorite endings, or favorite plot twists. While these aren't tropes in and of themselves, they may suggest tropes you might particularly enjoy.

7. What are the movies or TV shows you rewatch over and over and the books you've read so many times they're falling apart? Write down what you love most about those stories. Pay particular attention to the moments you tend to re-watch or re-read or include versions of in every story you imagine, plot, or write.

8. Jot down favorite foods, colors, weather, seasons, places— sky's the limit. The key is to capture many, many things you really, really like or that you repeat over and over in your life.

I keep a running list of these things in a spreadsheet on my computer, and I add to it as I discover new things that fascinate me. As of this writing, my list is over a thousand entries long. It includes things like horses, dogs, military men, spaghetti, rain, secret societies, and smart women in jeopardy.

I hear you pointing out, but these aren't tropes. Correct! (And yay for you understanding what a trope is already!) But, by looking through our lists of favorite things, we can find plenty of elements that are common to various tropes.

Let's take my love of secret societies, for example While that's not a trope in and of itself, a secret society might make an appearance in a hero-in-disguise trope, a reclusive hero trope, a secret identity trope, a secret world story, or perhaps a rescue story.

Spaghetti might lead me to thinking about a restaurant or maybe a big family dinner...and those might lead me to an employee-boss story of a chef on the hunt for the perfect spaghetti recipe and an Italian restaurant employee, or an other-side-of-the-tracks story about a person from a tiny family falling for a person from a huge family and spaghetti acting as a metaphor for love in this story.

1. Pick out something you're particularly drawn to from your list. Now, browse through this book (or the other volumes in my series) and search for tropes that might work well with that thing you love and that appeal to you to write.

2. If you're the ultra-organized type, you might start a second list of tropes that relate to things you love. They're likely to be tropes you'll find comfortable and enjoyable to write.

3. If you're a more spontaneous type, pick out something you're drawn to from your list and browse through this book with that thing in mind. I'll bet an idea (or several) for a story are triggered by some one of the tropes you explore. That's likely a trope you'll find to be a good fit if you sit down to play with it.

I can tell you with assurance, there are certain tropes that, no matter how much I might like something that relates closely to them, I will never, ever, be drawn to or want to write. You will find the same. The tropes you absolutely hate will not resonate with you, no matter what.

.   .   .

It's worth noting that the names of tropes can and do evolve over time, sometimes quite rapidly. In fact, historically, tropes were often referred to by the name of a classic character, fable, or even a nursery rhyme that perfectly illustrated that story arc. What was once called the Heathcliff trope has become the reclusive hero or brooding hero trope. The Frankenstein trope has become loving-a-monster or simply, monstrous lover trope.

In this book, I have chosen the most descriptive names I can come up with unless there is already a name so commonly used that just about everyone will automatically understand what it refers to.

Regardless of how a classic, universal trope is currently being labeled, the basic story will remain the same, unchanged, recognizable, and archetypal.

It's also important to note that some tropes lose their acceptability in cultural, societal, and political environments as those environments evolve and grow. While nobody thought twice about writing an enslaved hero or heroine several hundred years ago (or sadly, much more recently than that), this trope is not widely accepted as a positive trope to write about in contemporary fiction today. Likewise, writing a romance between an interracial couple several hundred years ago would have been highly controversial but is widely accepted today.

Side note: I chose the two examples in the previous paragraph as a blunt reminder of just how fraught certain tropes have the potential to be.

Secretary-boss romances can be a minefield in today's #MeToo environment. Makeover stories where the hero doesn't notice the heroine until she gets thin aren't likely to land well with most audience members today. **Just because a trope exists doesn't mean it is always appropriate or a good idea to write today**.

That said, I would never say never to any writer who wants to tackle a potentially difficult, touchy, or fraught trope in a story. It's always possible to tell a fantastic story with sensitivity, grace, an ethical perspective, and profound meaning regardless of the subject matter. Just be careful and be aware as you choose your tropes of the possible pitfalls of some of them.

Beyond their potential to offend readers and viewers, it's also worth noting that tropes simply come into and go out of fashion. Indeed, in today's world of rapid streaming TV/film releases and eBooks that can go from idea to published story in a matter of weeks, these shifts can happen at light speed, rising and falling in popularity in a matter of months or a few years.

The good news is classic love stories have been around since the beginning of time, and they'll continue to stick around until the end of time. What is old becomes new over and over. The story of Cleopatra resurfaces as modern reverse harem stories. The Taming of the Shrew? It has been reborn as today's Grumpy-Sunshine trope.

Perhaps the most classic example of all is the tale of Romeo and Juliet, which has been told over and over through the centuries since Shakespeare penned his star-crossed-lovers tale (and in it, actually coined the phrase, "star-cross'd lovers"). But, let the record show the star-crossed-lovers stories of Orpheus and Eurydice, Tristan and Isolde, Hou Yi and Chang'e, Achilles and Patroclus, and Panganoran and Magayon, all pre-dated Romeo and Juliet...some of them by a lot. Even Shakespeare himself was borrowing classic tropes and re-adapting them to his own time and audiences.

Today's rapid rise and fall in the popularity of various tropes creates an interesting opportunity for story creators. Every time a new and trendy trope comes along, a dedicated fan base builds around that trope. While the fans may get tired of binging on a particular trope, it's a good bet that in the long run a solid, core fanbase for that once-trendy trope will survive and thrive...even if that trope goes out of vogue as the hot new thing.

Indeed, various researchers have identified a cycle that book readers, in particular, tend to go through. In the first year of reading a particular type of fiction, they'll consume everything in sight. In the second year, they'll refine their tastes and start to be choosier about the stories they read...which is to say, they find their favorite tropes and begin to niche down more tightly in what they purchase to read. By the third year or so of being a dedicated book fan, readers know exactly what they like reading and they tend not to deviate from those types of stories for the long term.

I've never seen an academic study of how TV and film viewers choose their content, but I expect it's a similar arc of finding their favorite story types and sticking to them for the most part.

This tendency of tropes to come and go in popularity also means that, if you write fast and can bring your book or screenplay to market quickly, it's not a bad idea to write to the hot-trending tropes. (Assuming of course, that you don't have to write your trendy tale while trying all the while not to gag in disgust or break out laughing at the horrible implausibility of it.)

Readers and TV/film viewers are very perceptive and will spot in a second a project created by a writer who personally hates his or her subject matter. If you look closely, I suspect you'll be able to pick out which tropes in this book are not my cup of tea. I've done my best to disguise my personal biases, but we all have them.

The key in choosing a story that will resonate with readers or viewers and achieve popular success is to find the overlap between the stories you love and the ones the reading/viewing public currently loves.

If you find a trendy trope you love, but you happen to miss the big wave of its popularity, you can still write that trope and expect to find readers and viewers for it. You may have to wait for readers and viewers who are glutted on a certain story type to renew their hunger for that particular trope, but they *will* come back.

Tropes, once created, never really go away. They become an evergreen part of the collective consciousness of all people who consume stories in any format.

As you browse through this book, you'll see a definite pattern to how all romance tropes proceed. Readers and viewers also know that pattern. Even if they've never interacted with a specific trope before, they'll be pretty good at guessing where your story should go.

Almost without exception, all stories are built around a trope, or more often several tropes interwoven, that form the core structure of the story. We might even go so far as to say tropes are the individual vertebrae that form the backbones of all stories. They inform which scenes will be in your story and in what order they will happen. They are certainly the basis of the entire romance fiction industry.

At its most fundamental level, every love story ever written follows the trope of one sentient being meeting another sentient being, attraction forms, obstacles are overcome, and the beings end up together, usually happily ever after. Every single romance trope is some variation on that theme.

Tropes are one of the most important tools all writers use, knowingly or unknowingly, in constructing and delivering satisfying stories to their audience. And yet, they're little understood and often greatly misunderstood.

WHAT IS A TROPE?

Let's start at the beginning and talk about what a trope is.

The word trope originates from the ancient Greek work *trepein*, which means to turn, to direct, to alter, to change. *Trepein* evolved into the later Greek word *tropos*, which means turn, direction, way. Sometime in the 1530s, the Latin word *tropus* was first used to mean a turn of speech or figure of speech.

It is worth noting from these early definitions that the concept of a trope includes turns of direction and change. There's movement to tropes, and they don't follow a straight line. They connote action. Travel from one point to another.

Which is to say, **tropes are a roadmap of where a story must go. They're a way of marking certain scenes a story must contain, and they're a way of breaking**

down the plot of a story into its core elements. Tropes are the universal, archetypal arcs that underlie *every* story.

If you pop over to a modern dictionary to look trope up, you'll find something along the lines of "a figurative or metaphorical use of a word or expression." Secondarily, tropes are often defined as "a common or overused theme or device, a cliché."

However, this is not precisely what people in the publishing industry or TV/film industry mean when they use this word.

KEY POINT: In the context of literary works and screenplays, the word trope means "a commonly recurring literary or rhetorical device, motif or cliché in creative works."

Let's unpack that a bit. A trope is a theme, arc, or plot device that runs throughout a story, and that is used repeatedly in many stories by many writers. Star crossed lovers, taming the bad boy, enemies to lovers, secret babies—they've been around since the very first stories were told in the distant mists of time and human speech.

How many ancient cavemen came back to their cave after a hard day of hunting and gathering, and by speech, sign language, or pantomime told the story, "There I was, taking a walk with my mate. And all of a sudden, a saber-toothed tiger jumped out of the bushes right in front of us. And then I..."

Or how many ancient cavewomen relayed to their friends, "I was out all day, hunting and gathering berries. And when I came back to the cave, you'll never guess who I caught Ogg messing around with on our skins. And then I..."

While I have no idea if primitive homo sapiens told these exact tales, you get the point. These stories, hero/heroine-in-jeopardy and cheating spouse, have been around as long as storytelling has existed, are universally related to and immediately understood by all people, and have reflected the human experience for as long as we've had the ability to share them.

Moreover, we tell these same classic, universal stories over and over, even today. Story tropes resonate down through history from Ogg the caveman, to Greek theater, to Chaucer's Tales, to Shakespeare's plays, to the development of the fiction novel, right on down to modern commercial fiction in its many and varied forms of delivery to the consumer.

These recurring arcs and plot themes that shape a story are what make up that elusive thing called trope.

WHAT TROPE ISN'T

Writers often confuse story elements with tropes. Take, for example a meet cute. I often see this described as a trope. While the hero and heroine meeting in a fun and creative way draws in the audience quickly and effectively, in and of itself, it doesn't tell the reader or viewer a single thing about where the story is going. Will this be a secretary-boss romance? An opposites attract story? An other-side of-the -tracks or bad boy/girl reformed story?

The almost-left-behind hero/heroine, the big secret revealed, forgiveness granted, or sparks flying are all STORY elements but not tropes that suggest fully developed story arcs. By themselves none of these elements tell the reader a thing about the type of story they're reading or where the story is going to end up.

Writers often confuse a character theme with a trope, as well. A character theme is some attribute that describes a character. It often affects the story significantly, but it is not the source of twists, turns, and movement, the active plot if you will, of the story.

EXAMPLE:

A widow is not a trope. A widow learning how to love again is.

A shapeshifter is not a trope. A shapeshifter fated to love a human is.

A bride is not a trope. A bride left at the altar and struggling to love again is.

A cowboy is not a trope. A cowboy displaced to a big city and learning to fit in is.

Take the example of the cowboy. The fact that the hero is a cowboy may greatly color the mood and setting of your story, and the cowboy as hero comes with a ready-made set of props that the reader or viewer will absolutely expect to see.

Every historical cowboy must be accompanied by horses, and well, cows. Stetsons, spurs, six-shooters, saloons, and maybe a barmaid with a heart of gold would not be remiss. A modern cowboy may have traded in his horse for a pick-up truck or even a helicopter. Props aside, however, that essentially honorable, nature-loving, rough-around-the-edges loner remains.

And yet, for all the flavor a cowboy hero brings to any story, his existence alone does not give the story any movement or create any expectations for the reader of what conflicts and resolution lie ahead for our intrepid cowboy. That job belongs to the trope.

Will our cowboy have to fight off some threat to his ranch from a dastardly neighbor bent on stealing his herd or his land? Will our cowboy find a woman with no memory wandering on his land and take her in? Will our cowboy find himself stranded in a blizzard at the cabin of his attractive young widow neighbor? Will our cowboy be forced to move to a big city to build a new life?

The tropes in the previous paragraph—saving his home, amnesia, stranded with a stranger, and fish out of water—are what will give our cowboy's story movement, a problem to solve, and a logical, predictable story structure. These tropes will let our reader know what to expect from this cowboy's story.

Why do we care if the reader has any idea of what to expect from a story?

I'll say it again because it bears repeating. **One of the great paradoxes of fiction reading and TV/film viewing is that audience members don't want to be surprised, at least not in the large-scale movements that form the core of the story.**

When readers pick up a romance novel or viewers watch a romantic movie, they by golly expect the two main characters to end up together at the end of the story. Furthermore, they also expect a happily ever after unless you've specifically signaled to the reader/viewer up front that they're headed toward a more ambiguous happily for now ending.

If a reader picks up a mystery novel, he or she expects the mystery to be solved by the end of the story. Spy thriller movie? The world must be saved before the final credits roll. Crime thriller? Justice had better be served.

Likewise, readers and viewers have definite expectations of how the smaller arcs that form an overall story will progress and resolve. If the cowboy's ranch is threatened, the reader/viewer absolutely expects that, after some scary threats and nearly losing the ranch, our cowboy hero will find a way to save his home. If our cowboy gets stranded in a blizzard with a beautiful widow, the story consumer expects attraction to unfold as they're forced to get to know each other and work together to survive. Indeed, the reader/viewer also expects the storm to lift eventually and the cowboy and his widow to realize they want to stay together forever, even after life resumes its normal course.

KEY POINT: If you, the writer, don't deliver on the reader's or viewer's expectations of how a trope will unfold and resolve in your story, the reader/viewer will

be outraged. Outraged readers and viewers have an unpleasant tendency to leave terrible reviews, tell everyone they know how awful your story was, and never buy another book or watch another TV show or film you've created.

When you introduce any trope into a story, a specific set of problems is inevitably bound to occur as a result of that trope and require a specific resolution.

Returning to our cowboy, misplaced into a big city this time, he's out of his natural environment and must either learn to fit in or make his environment fit him. Note that in this case, two possible outcomes are suggested. This particular trope is somewhat more flexible than some other tropes. But still, certain, specific conflicts and resolutions are required by this trope.

An important side note, the names that tropes are commonly given can be a bit confusing. Because they get discussed so often within the publishing and TV/film industries, there's a tendency to shorten the full descriptions of tropes into familiar nicknames.

EXAMPLE: Childhood sweethearts. In and of itself, the fact that two characters were once childhood sweethearts doesn't connote a classic story type or inevitable plot points. More accurately, we would call this trope, "childhood sweethearts reunite and fall in love as adults." But that's clumsy and a mouthful to say every time you mention it. Most people will refer to it simply as a childhood sweethearts trope. The rest of it is generally understood.

If you're confused as to whether something is a character theme or an actual trope, ask yourself, does the fact that a person has a specific characteristic or problem suggest an entire story arc? If the answer is no, it's merely a character theme. If the answer is yes, it's a trope.

EXAMPLE: Your hero is a Scottish highlander. What has to happen because he's a highlander? We have no idea. Perhaps the English will seize his lands. Perhaps a feisty lass he grew up with will win over his heart. Perhaps he'll go raiding and kidnap himself a Sassenach bride. We have no idea where the story is headed, simply because the hero is a highlander. It only tells us he's likely to wear a kilt and speak with a brogue. So, highlander hero is not a trope.

WHY BOTHER WITH TROPES?

In the first place, you're not likely to avoid them altogether in any story you tell. Tropes are so baked into every book you've ever read, every television show or movie you've ever watched, even the casual verbal stories we share with other people, that you can hardly avoid them if you try.

We can even go so far as to say that our actual lives are a series of tropes, many of them universal to all human beings: growing up, falling in love, making a living, possibly raising a family or finding an intentional family, growing old, and dying. The many challenges common to all of us that form the conflicts, obstacles, tragedies, and triumphs of our lives are the stuff of tropes. We're all familiar with them. They resonate throughout all our lives.

One reason we read books and watch television and movies is to vicariously overcome these challenges as we live in the skin of the main characters of a story for a little while. We learn how to deal with the tropes of our own lives. We make peace with the tropes we've struggled through. We learn from the hard lessons other (fictional or real) people have learned by hearing about the challenges posed by the tropes in their lives.

Occasionally, authors brag that they've written books without tropes. I've even heard a publisher demand trope-free books or a producer ask for trope-free screenplays from time to time. The truth is, writing without tropes is simply not possible if you expect to tell a story that sets up a dilemma or conflict of any kind and resolves it in the end.

Tropes are the beginnings, middles, and endings of story arcs, the predictable and logical progressions from a starting place to an ending place in a plot.

When a publisher or producer asks for a trope-free story, my guess is they're actually asking for a cliché-free plot. At a minimum, what they're asking for is a unique or rarely used trope, or perhaps a unique twist upon a traditional trope.

Let's face it. A romance is a trope all by itself. In its simplest form, boy meets girl (or some combination of interchangeable genders), there's attraction, there's conflict, there's happily ever after. Boom. A trope.

In publishers' and producers' defense, because tropes get used over and over by writers of all stripes across all genres and mediums of storytelling, it can be challenging to write a book or screenplay that feels new, fresh, and different from every other story that relies on the same tropes.

In fact, the word "trope" has come to be synonymous with cliché-laden writing. I would argue this has much more to do with tropes being written badly, packaged badly, and overused than with what tropes actually are.

The second reason to bother with tropes is that readers and viewers are trained to expect and look for tropes, and in fact, psychologists suggest that audiences crave the familiarity of tropes in their story-based entertainment. Why else would readers and viewers return to the same tropes over and over?

Lisa Cron puts it brilliantly in <u>Wired for Story</u> when she says,

"We think in story. It's hardwired in our brain. It's how we make strategic sense of the otherwise overwhelming world around us."

I would take that one-step further and propose that not only do we think in story, but more specifically, we also think in tropes. Tropes are the building blocks of story, the sub-stories within the larger story that give our lives—and books, TV shows, and movies—shape and substance. Tropes occur in an orderly fashion, and they show us the logical progression of events that must happen for a particular kind of story to reach a satisfying conclusion.

EXAMPLE: A secretary falls in love with her boss. The only logical path forward for our beleaguered and ignored secretary to find happiness with her oh-so-attractive employer is for her to finally get the boss's attention, gain his romantic interest, overcome any obstacles presented by being his employee and by the work environment around them, and to persevere until that man puts a ring on her finger.

There's no other reasonable path forward to a positive conclusion for our secretary and her boss. In the absence of any of those steps, a happy outcome is thrown into serious doubt, and in fact, not likely to happen at all.

She never gains his attention? No way for romance to unfold. He's not interested when he does notice her? Not likely to move forward into a satisfying romance. Obstacles in the workplace can't be overcome? No way to ethically become a couple. No ring on the finger? Honey, that jerk is just taking advantage of you.

Tropes certainly have variations and can take differing paths to happily ever after. And of course, if your goal is to write a tragedy rather than a happy story, tropes can lead to a failed romance.

But at their core, these love stories *all* have a predictable beginning, middle, and end. **If you want to satisfy your audience,**

you must give them all the parts of each trope in your story.

The third reason to bother learning about tropes and how to use them effectively is they are an incredibly powerful and useful tool for working writers.

- If you understand tropes thoroughly, your story's plot will unfold before you effortlessly (well, with somewhat less blood, sweat, and tears).
- Your characters will know what to do next when the sagging middle of your book is yawning before you like the Grand Canyon with the happy ending only a distant speck on the far side of the chasm.
- And best of all, you will deliver a deeply satisfying story to your audience.

OBLIGATORY SCENES

One of the great beauties—and pitfalls—of tropes is that they all require certain major scenes to happen, usually in a specific order, to tell that particular story motif. If you're writing about a kidnapped heroine, she a) must be kidnapped, b) must be in danger of not being rescued, and c) be rescued.

- **Every single trope has a logical starting point or inciting event.**
- **Every single trope has a logical middle that takes the form of an obstacle or conflict preventing its successful resolution.**

- **Every single trope has a specific black moment where all appears to be lost in a way unique to that particular trope.**
- **Every single trope has a logical and satisfying conclusion.**

When a writer creates a story, he or she enters into an unspoken contract with the reader or viewer. The writer agrees to deliver the story the reader/viewer expects. This contract also extends to the tropes the writer employs in the story.

If you break this contract with your reader/viewer, that consumer will not forgive you. Trust me. I've seen the hate mail and verbal attacks readers and viewers spew in fury at writers who break this contract.

KEY POINT: You must not fail to deliver the logical and satisfying conclusion your reader or viewer expects from the tropes in your story. Never, EVER, fail to deliver on the promise of the tropes you use.

Filmmaker, Stanley Kubrick said, "Everything has already been done, every story has been told, every scene has been shot. It's our job to do it one better."

Every trope has been used thousands or even millions of times. But they continue to exist because we love them. Why do we love them so much? They're universally recognizable and familiar to all of us.

They're old friends; we grew up with them. We've listened to and learned these classic tropes since we could understand speech. They help us understand the world around us. And, in the case of romance tropes, they teach us logical ways to overcome universal, classic obstacles to love.

Another important reason we all love tropes is because they inevitably lead our hero and heroine—who are, of course, alter egos for the reader or viewer himself or herself—to achieve universally appealing dreams, wishes, or fantasies.

Who doesn't wish to be plucked from poverty and whisked into a life of wealth and ease? Who doesn't wish to be waited on hand and foot, or to be given a gift of great value, to be popular, to find one's tribe, or to be the one chosen to be loved out of all possible love interests?

Tropes *work* for the exact same reason we love them. We recognize them. We find them comforting and familiar. We have a deep-seated need to see each trope work out happily.

Your job as a writer is to put into action what Kubrick said. You must find a way to take what is old and make it new. You must tell your story in your own voice, with your own perspective, while remaining true to the time-honored tropes you choose to use.

I can't tell you how many times I've asked editors, or heard other writers ask producers, or even heard writers ask their fans, "What book/show/movie are you looking for, right now?"

The answer is always some version of, "I want the same story that has always worked before and that I've loved in the past, but new and fresh. Different but the same."

I also can't tell you how many times I've pulled out my own hair over that answer or listened to other writers wail in frustration over it. Different but the same? What the heck does that mean?

Let me translate for you. Editors, producers, readers, and viewers want the classic tropes they've always loved and that have always appealed to them but told in a fresh, new way that makes them enjoy the trope all over again.

One last piece of advice about using tropes: it is easy to write mechanically when focused solely on trope, marching grimly through the obligatory scenes of a trope, never varying, never embellishing, never reaching for anything more. The most boring book or movie in the world is one that relies solely on tropes to define the story. However, the best book or movie in the world can also rely solely on tropes to define and tell a story.

Assuming all the requirements of a trope are met, quality of writing is not defined by using tropes or not using tropes, but rather how skillfully the writer uses them.

3

HOW TO USE THIS BOOK

This book covers internal tropes that are universal to all sub-genres of romance, meaning they're adaptable to any type of romantic story, or even to a romantic sub-plot in a book or screenplay that's not primarily a romance. The entire romance fiction genre, which is very large, is usually divided into a series of sub-genres, including but by no means limited to:

-- historical romance

-- romantic suspense

-- contemporary romance

-- paranormal romance

-- sweet romance

-- romantic comedy

-- small town romance

-- inspirational romance

-- and so on...

All the tropes analyzed in this book can be applied to stories in *any* of these genres. There are many more tropes specific to individual sub-genres, of course. A forced marriage might work perfectly well in an historical romance, but it would struggle to translate well into a sweet, contemporary romance or a romantic comedy, for example. I have not included those genre-specific tropes in these volumes relating specifically to universal romance tropes. (And yes, I promise to write a series of books dealing with genre-specific romance tropes.)

It is not uncommon to combine a romance trope with a trope(s) from another genre of fiction to create a crossover project. For example, a romantic thriller, fantasy romance, or a romantic mystery.

It's also entirely possible that these classic romance tropes can be borrowed by other genres of film and fiction and appear in young adult projects, science fiction projects, mysteries, and thrillers, to name a few. In fact, they can appear in any form of television/film/fiction/other story formats where two characters in the story fall in love after overcoming some sort of obstacle(s).

Overview of this Book

As you've seen, each trope description in this book includes:

- a definition of the trope
- adjacent tropes
- why readers/viewers love this particular trope
- a list of the obligatory scenes that form the beginning, middle, black moment, and end of the trope's arc
- any additional scenes that are key to doing this trope justice
- a list of questions to consider when writing this trope
- a list of potential hazards and pitfalls of writing this trope
- examples of movies and books that use this trope

In some cases, several tropes may be closely related. They may describe varying degrees of the same trait in a character, for example: Reclusive Hero, Shy Hero, and Socially Awkward Hero. Or tropes may be variations on the same idea, for example: Dangerous Secret, Secret Baby, Secret Marriage, Secret Identity. Or tropes may contain adjacent story elements or themes, for example: Love Triangle, Best Friend's Sibling, Ménage, Harem.

In these cases when tropes overlap or descriptions of one may help you develop another similar or related trope, feel free to refer to similar tropes as you refine your primary trope or if you want to expand beyond the strict confines of a specific trope.

At the end of this book, I have included an appendix listing all the universal romance tropes and which volume in the Universal Romance Tropes series they appear in.

If you already have some idea of the trope or tropes you'd like to write about, you can go directly to those specific descriptions for inspiration and thought-provoking questions as you plotters plan your story or you pantsers ruminate on the possibilities you might like to explore.

For those of you unfamiliar with the terms, plotters are those writers who like to fully plan and outline a story before they commence writing it. Pantsers are writers who prefer to sit down and begin writing without planning much or any of the story in advance. Rather, pantsers write by the seat of their pants, organically letting the story unfold as the characters and story dictate in the moment.

Many writers are some combination of the two.

There is NO right or wrong way to write your story. Whatever works for you is the best and right way for you to develop your story. The good news is this book is designed to be useful to both plotters and pantsers.

Plotters are likely to refer to this book during the planning process and before beginning to write as a tool for developing story, characters, and scenes. Pantsers may be more inclined to use this book as an idea generator either in the story development phase or when stuck on what to do next. Pantsers may also use this book to develop a very general idea of characters and/or where your story is going before sitting down to write.

All writers can use this book effectively during or after the drafting process to check their work against the expectations of the tropes that they've planned or that have emerged over the course of drafting their story.

If you've already drafted a story using particular tropes, you can go directly to those trope descriptions to get revision and editing ideas and to ensure you've delivered the kind of story your reader will expect...and more importantly, that your reader will LOVE.

If you've written a story and you're considering how to market it, you can also use this book as a guide to figure out which classic trope(s) your story best fits. You can check to make sure your marketing and advertising materials—title, logline, tagline, blurb, trailer, back cover copy—are properly tailored to signal your story's particular trope(s) to prospective consumers of your story.

HELPFUL HINT: The idea behind signaling in your marketing materials which tropes will be in your story is not to draw every reader or viewer to your story but rather to attract the readers and viewers who will absolutely love the tropes in your story. They'll get a satisfying experience, you'll get positive reviews, and you'll gain a loyal fan who trusts you to deliver the story you promised. Most importantly, you'll gain a repeat customer.

If you're in the early planning stages of a story, or you're simply looking for an idea to spark a new story, this book is a useful tool for you as well.

HOW TO USE TROPE TO BUILD STORY

While plotting vs. pantsing describes how a writer develops story, what they think of first when developing story divides writers into two more categories.

In my experience, there are two kinds of writers in this world: character-driven writers who think in characters and develop characters first when creating a story, and plot-driven writers who think in events and action and develop plot first when creating a story.

As writers gain experience, over time and multiple projects, we all become more adept at thinking in terms of both character development and plot development as we prepare to write a new story. However, we all have a default setting that is our first, natural, and probably strongest skill in the story planning process.

Tropes can be one of, if not the most, powerful tools in *both* types of writers' story planning processes. Understanding tropes allows all writers to make sure they are creating fully realized plots *and* fully realized characters that will be satisfying to readers or viewers.

Many years ago, I participated in a continuity project at a major publishing house. Twelve authors were given a bible created by the publisher that described twelve linked stories, and each of us was assigned to write one novel in the series. It so happened that the heroine I was assigned was the sister of a heroine in another book in the series.

The author of the sister's book called me shortly after we all got to work on our books because she wanted to develop her heroine's back story and wanted to make sure the family and family issues she built for her heroine would also work as backstory for my heroine.

Now, I should confess here that I am naturally a plot-driven writer. It quickly became obvious that the other author I was speaking with was a character-driven writer. I opened the conversation by saying to her, "Tell me a little about the story you're thinking of writing."

She launched enthusiastically into a description of her heroine's hopes and dreams, fears and failures. She talked about wanting to write angst between the heroine and her father, and how hard it was going to be for the heroine to trust the hero because of that.

After about thirty seconds of her talking in this vein, I interrupted the author to ask, "Yes, but what does she *do*? What *happens* in your story?"

The lovely author went silent for a moment, obviously taken aback by the question, and finally said, "Tell me about your story."

I enthusiastically launched into telling her how my heroine stumbled across evidence of a plot to assassinate the president, went to a prison to question a terrorist where she got caught in the middle of a prison break, had to escape that, make her way to the White House, get a Secret Service agent to listen to her, try to find the bad guys—

And at about that point, the other author interrupted my tale of action, adventure, and danger to ask, "Yes, but how does she *feel*?"

I should probably add that my mind went completely blank and I had no idea how to answer that question. At that time in my career, I didn't typically figure out how my characters felt until I was actually writing (or sometimes, revising) the scene.

The moral of this story is that those two simple questions fully encompass both the plotting and character aspects of writing. You must answer *both* questions in the course of writing your story. Furthermore, in every major scene of your story, these same questions must be answered if you're to give your readers a satisfying experience.

Every single obligatory scene must answer these two questions:

But what do they do?
But how do they feel?

. . .

So, how can both character-driven writers and plot-driven writers use tropes to help plan and flesh out their story, and to be sure to answer these two vital questions?

DEVELOPING PLOT FROM TROPE

Often, writers have no trouble developing interesting, multi-layered characters with fascinating back stories and unique individual qualities. But once this fabulous cast of characters has taken shape, the writer must figure out what on earth to DO with them to carry an entire novel or screenplay.

Enter your friend the trope.

Take a look at the characters you've already played around with and browse through this book until you find several tropes that would challenge your wonderful and fascinating main characters and force them into either a personal transformation or into a relationship they must find a way to transform into a happily ever after.

ROMANTIC TRAGEDIES

Yes, I'm aware that not all love stories end in happily ever after. Many stories still classed as romances end more ambiguously in a happily for now or a sort-of happy. And of course, tragic love stories end in a failed relationship or worse. Cue the Romeo and Juliet theme music.

For the purposes of describing tropes in this series of books, I have chosen to describe a positive outcome to the love story built by each trope. **All that's necessary to convert *any* of these tropes to a negative outcome (a romantic tragedy) is simply to reverse the positive outcome of the 'ENDING' obligatory scene**.

Interestingly enough, the rest of the obligatory scenes of the trope will usually remain pretty much the same. The characters will meet, fall in love, be faced with an obstacle or series of obstacles that become ever more challenging and difficult.

The lovers will arrive at a black moment where all appears to be lost...so far, we're tracking along pretty much exactly beside the lovers who get a positive outcome...but then, in the ENDING of the romantic tragedy, the lovers' climactic efforts to overcome the black moment fail. Boom. Tragedy complete.

In point of technical fact, I could title this series The Tropoholic's Guide to Universal Romance and Romantic Tragedy. But that's even longer and more of a mouthful than the current title, so I'll just stick with what I've got.

All plot in all types of romance stories, both happy and sad, is a journey of change—of two people starting in one place and ending up in another—a place that makes happily ever after not only possible but fully realized, makes their tragic failure to find love complete and devastating, or someplace somewhere in between the two extremes.

EXERCISE: FINDING PLOT FROM EXISTING CHARACTERS, USING TROPES

Divide a sheet of paper or your computer screen in half, vertically. Label the left-hand column, BEFORE. Label the right-hand column, AFTER. In the before column, write down a list of main qualities or beliefs your hero possesses, both good and bad, at the start of your story.

Now, beside each of those words, in the AFTER column write down the opposite of each quality or belief. You have just mapped a very simple set of change arcs for your hero from the BEFORE quality to the AFTER quality.

· · ·

Ask yourself the following questions about each pair of descriptive words:

1. What situation, crisis, or realization could cause the hero to shift from the BEFORE word to the AFTER word in a story?

2. Does the AFTER word represent a negative quality, which is to say a black moment (when the hero has lost everything, failed utterly, or fallen back into his worst, old ways)? Or does the AFTER word represent the hero's growth, change for the better, or overcoming his worst flaws, which is to say, a happy ending.

3. Now, keeping in mind your list of negative/black moment words in the AFTER column, browse through the trope descriptions in this book. Look for qualities in the black moments described in the book that match the black moment your hero might experience if he changes for the worse.

4. Likewise, look at your hero's AFTER words that represent growth and positive change, and browse through the endings of the various tropes in this book to find possible matches to your hero if he were to get his happily ever after.

5. You should now have a short list of possible tropes to use in your story that will illustrate your hero's change and growth over the course of your book.

6. Repeat this entire exercise for your heroine. See if any tropes in your two short lists match up to *both* your hero and heroine as you've designed them. Those tropes are obvious plot fits for the characters you've created. **It's fine, by the way, to write a separate trope for each of your main love interests in your story**.

7. Tweak both your hero and heroine's main qualities as needed to find a trope or tropes that work for both of them.

8. Pick a trope that sounds fun to write and start plotting how the obligatory events of that trope will force your hero and heroine to change and grow until they finally find true love. Or pick a couple of tropes that sound fun to play with and commence torturing your hero and heroine!

It's worth pointing out that the above exercise is in no way mandatory. If you already know what trope(s) you want to write in your story, by all means, dive right in. This exercise is purely meant to help you narrow down possible tropes if you have a hero and heroine in mind and have no idea where to begin with creating a plot for them.

Once you've picked a trope or a few tropes that will work for your characters and that you would enjoy writing, it's time to take a look at the obligatory scenes of the tropes you've chosen. What would each of those scenes look like in a story containing your main characters, in the genre or sub-genre you're writing, in the setting you've chosen?

Next, you need to ask yourself what preparatory or lead-up scenes are necessary in your story to set up those big obligatory scenes?

If you're planning to use more than one trope in your story, you will have to include all the obligatory scenes from all those tropes in your story. You may end up with anywhere from four to a dozen or more beginning, middle, black moment, and ending scenes that *must* be in your book to set up and follow through on your chosen tropes.

As an aside, if you've chosen to use more than one closely related trope in your story, several of these obligatory scenes may actually overlap or end up being the same scene. All this means is you've got one less obligatory scene that has to be included in your book.

Of course, it's vital that, if you have an obligatory scene that's pulling double duty as a key scene for more than one trope, it still has to satisfy the requirements of *both* tropes.

Now, take a look at the list of obligatory scenes you've made and ask yourself the following questions:

1. What other scenes will be necessary to include in your story to set up each of these obligatory scenes? These lead-up scenes will share critical information with the reader, build tension that climaxes in one of your obligatory scenes, describe the events and actions that move your characters toward the next obligatory scene.

2. What additional scenes are necessary to explain to the reader how and why the main characters will evolve, and move, from one obligatory scene to the next?

3. What scenes are necessary to raise the stakes for both characters and make your readers/viewers care deeply about them as they move from one obligatory scene to the next?

4. What scenes are necessary to demonstrate how your characters feel about and react to the obligatory scene that just took place?

Once you've brainstormed through these questions for each set of obligatory scenes from each trope you've chosen, you should be getting close to having a complete major scene list for your entire story.

Now that you've got a list of major scenes, you can fill out the rest of your plot with the minor scenes that not only set up the major scenes, but also lend flavor, humor, emotion, context, romantic attraction, secondary characters, and key elements of the genre you're writing.

For example, if you're writing a steamy contemporary romance, not only will major scenes need to reflect this, but the minor scenes will also need to establish and support the steam heat and help raise the temperature level of the overall story. If you're writing a comedy, both the minor and major scenes will need to establish and support the humor.

At any rate, after listing out all of your obligatory scenes, major scenes, and minor scenes, you should have a fairly complete scene list for your entire story.

Because I see you running screaming from pre-plotting a book, my pantser colleagues, you still *must* include each and every obligatory scene from whatever trope your book ends up being built around. Whether you do that in your first draft or you have to go back and revise the obligatory scenes into your final project, you still have to get every obligatory scene of your trope(s) into your story.

While I would never wish to interfere in the organic pantsing process, there is value in at least having some idea of the major story points (the obligatory scenes) you should be aiming toward including in your project.

Many pantser-writers I know do go ahead and pick a specific trope or set of tropes before they begin writing their stories. They use the list of obligatory scenes included in this book as guideposts for their journey. They pants their way from the beginning to the middle, from the middle to the black moment, and from there to the ending, but always with the next obligatory scene in mind as a target to get to...by whatever circuitous route the characters and plot ultimately take to get there.

If even this minimal amount of pre-set plot is too much for you, by all means, go ahead and draft your entire story by the seat of your pants. But once you've got a draft in hand and have identified the trope(s) you ended up using in your story, you must go back in the revision and editing phase and make sure you have included all of the obligatory scenes required by your story's trope(s).

I've been told that adding in obligatory scenes to a completed draft can be a nightmare of epic proportions. It typically requires extensive rejiggering of the plot and can cause major direction changes for characters that force extensive rewrites.

Even if you're a pure pantser, as soon as you get some idea of what trope(s) you may be leaning toward as your story unfolds, it's worth taking a peek at that trope's description to give yourself some idea of where you might want to head with the story and what the obligatory scenes might look like.

DEVELOPING CHARACTERS FROM TROPE

If you're the kind of writer who develops plot first and then creates characters to fit the story you plan to tell, tropes are your friend, as well. You, however, are likely to start your story planning process with this book rather than end your revision process with it.

Browse this book and the other volumes in this series...my apologies for the shameless plug...until you find one or several tropes that capture your imagination and sound like fun to build into a story.

Side note: I'm a big proponent of writers actually enjoying what they write. To quote the great Ann Maxwell, who wrote as Elizabeth Lowell, "It's very hard to write a wonderful story if you're typing with one hand and holding your nose with the other."

When you tell your story with joy and passion, it inevitably shows through in the words that end up on the page. Although I've given it a lot of thought over the years, and many of my students have asked me how to mechanically insert this sense of joy into a project of theirs, I can't give you a specific reason why it happens or describe how your passion comes through in the words you choose. But trust me. It does.

It's one of those mysteries of writing that ranks right up there with how a writer's voice comes across on the page. As far as I can tell, it has to do with the words you choose and the rhythms and cadences of the words you choose. But if you *love* the story you write, those who read your project *will* know it.

For my screenwriter colleagues, I realize you're at the mercy of directors and actors to share the same love of your story and ultimately to convey their passion and joy for your story to the viewing audience. But long before that happens, every agent, producer, studio scout/executive, investor, and creative person considering attaching to your project needs to feel your passion for your story.

You can't write a joyless, passionless screenplay and assume that someone along the way will inject passion for the project into your story. For that matter, you can't expect anyone to invest millions of dollars in your project in hopes that someone along the way in development will breathe life into your story. That's up to you.

Okay. So, you've found a few tropes that sound fun. Perhaps you already have a story premise in mind, maybe a hook that will start the story, or you've envisioned a big ending that would be fun to build up to. Maybe you have an entire plot developed already.

With all of these ideas in mind, browse the trope descriptions until you find several that will fit with the story you're planning to tell.

.   .   .

HELPFUL HINT: It's actually fine to choose tropes that don't seem to be a natural fit for the story you have in mind. Sometimes the unexpected trope creates a fascinating story with unusual conflicts for the hero and heroine to overcome. Drop a secret baby into a spy thriller. Maybe a marriage of convenience collides with your gothic mystery. Strand a bride or groom at the altar in your sci-fi fantasy tale. The beauty of these universal romance tropes is they'll translate to any love story in any setting. That's what makes them universal.

Once you've chosen the tropes for your story, write down a list of the obligatory scenes required by your tropes. Add in any other scenes you already know you want to work into your story. Write down the major events you know have to be in your story and the other events that have to happen to set up each of those major events and obligatory scenes.

Now, you have to populate those scenes with human beings. Ask yourself the following questions:

1. What kind of hero/heroine would be **best** suited to do the all the things your rough plot outline requires of them? There's going to be a shootout? Do you need a police officer or an ex-soldier as your hero?

2. What kind of hero/heroine would be **worst** suited to do all the things your rough plot outline requires of them? Don't be afraid to throw your hero and heroine into situations way over their heads to handle. Force them to reach beyond what they think they're capable of. Force them to grow. Maybe that climactic shootout would be

more interesting with a pacifist or a scared-to-death-of-guns kindergarten teacher as your hero.

3. What are the emotional stakes baked into in each of the tropes you've chosen? What kind of character will find these emotional stakes difficult to embrace? Deeply meaningful? Painful? Challenging? Worth risking everything to achieve?

4. How will the hero and heroine change as a result of the tropes you've chosen? What is their beginning point and end point in the story based on these tropes? Will this be a journey of emotional transformation? Personal redemption? A change in understanding or attitude?

Once you've made a bunch of notes for yourself based on these questions, map out an arc for each main character where he or she moves from the starting points of the tropes you've chosen to the obligatory ending of each.

EXERCISE: FINDING CHARACTER ARC FROM TROPES

1. Once you have a list of the major scenes in your book, take a piece of paper and divide it in half vertically, or divide a computer screen vertically. Label the left-hand column, BEFORE, and label the right-hand column, AFTER.

2. You might want to number your scenes for convenience's sake. Now, for scene number one, write down in a few words or short phrases how your hero feels before the scene starts.

3. How does he feel about himself?
4. How does he feel about the heroine?
5. How does he feel about the situation in this scene before it starts?
6. How does he feel about this situation after this scene takes place?
7. What has going through this situation changed about the hero?

1. Repeat answering these questions for each major scene in your story. If you don't already know how the hero feels as he progresses through each of the major scenes, think in terms of progress, change, and growth toward a final lesson learned or a final and irrevocable change for the better in your hero that makes him able to love fully and completely.
2. Take a look at the hero's changes from major scene to major scene. Is there an overall arc of change? It's worth noting that there should be setbacks along the way, reversals of course, moments when he doubts himself, and moments when he rejects or refuses to take the next emotional step of change and growth. If you don't have the setbacks in his arc, build some in, now. Look at places in the plot where things can go badly for the hero and give him these setbacks.
3. Repeat this entire exercise for the heroine in the second column of your paper or screen.
4. By now, you have a list of how the events of the story affect your hero and heroine and drive their progress toward achieving their happily ever afters.
5. Now, ask yourself the question, how, as these events take place, can the heroine help along or actually cause the

hero's change/growth/setback in that scene to take place? Vice versa, how can the hero cause the heroine's change/growth/setback in that scene to take place?

You should have a bunch of notes now about how the movement, the action if you will, of your story—the trope—shapes and defines your characters' growth and change throughout the story.

It's all well and good for the events of the plot to force the hero and heroine to grow and change. But at the end of the day, you're writing a love story (even if it's only a subordinate plotline in a larger, non-romantic story). The hero and heroine themselves should also be drivers of teaching their partner the lessons and skills they need to become ideally suited for each other. Hence, the final question in the exercise above of how the hero and heroine affect and shape each other over the course of the story.

With that in mind, add into your plot-based scene list additional scenes that are needed to show your hero and heroine in conflict emotionally and beginning to address and resolve their emotional conflicts.

Then, go back one more time and add in any additional scenes needed to capture more emotional notes of tenderness, sadness, humor. Add in whatever scenes you need to flesh out how they *feel*, to paint the heat level of their relationship, to add secondary characters who aid and abet or try to foil the hero and heroine's romance, and show the required elements of the genre you're writing in.

Helpful Hint: There is no right or wrong way to develop story. Use whatever method works best for you. Characters can shape the plot, or plot can shape the charac-

ters, or some combination of both. But in all cases, the glue that holds characters and plot together and makes sure they travel a logical path together to a satisfying resolution is the story's trope(s). The plot is shaped by the tropes you choose, and those tropes will shape the emotional journeys taken by your characters.

LAYERING TROPES

In the shorter written romance story formats and in screenplays (particularly where the romance is a B plot), it's not uncommon to zero in on a single main trope to carry the entire story arc. In fact, it can make sense to stick to a single trope within the constraints of a smaller word count or page count.

The shorter the book or screenplay, the less room there is to interweave—and do justice to—multiple tropes. After all, for each additional trope you include in your story, the number of obligatory scenes goes up.

For some tropes, however, the obligatory scenes may overlap considerably. This can reduce the overall number of obligatory scenes enough to shorten the overall length of a novel or screenplay.

Example: A left at the altar bride trope is layered with a redemption trope, and the groom who jilted her spends the story trying to earn back her trust.

In establishing why the groom left her at the altar in the first place, you're also establishing the starting point for your hero's redemption arc. Leaving his fiancée at the altar may be the very thing (or the outward symptom of the very thing) he's got to come back from.

The triumphant personal growth moment of the heroine finally moving on with her life is also the black moment for the hero as his attempt at redeeming himself in her eyes seems to have utterly failed.

The hero's triumphant personal moment of finally proving he's worthy to the heroine is also the obligatory resolution moment of the bride's left at the altar trope where she finally finds a man who will be steadfast and never, ever leave her.

Any number of universal romance tropes lend themselves to this heavy layering and intermingling of obligatory scenes. Other combinations of tropes, however, will require distinct and separate resolutions of each trope before the happy ever after ending can be achieved.

The kidnapped heroine must be rescued before she can get her fairy tale wedding to her knight in shining armor. The hero's devastating secret must be revealed before the burned-by love, distrusting heroine can take the leap of faith and agree to marry him.

Particularly in the case where a trope from another genre of fiction is blended with a romance trope, the need for distinct and separate endings often becomes more pronounced. The evil empire must be defeated before the intrepid space cowboy gets the girl. The psychopathic murderer must be captured before the hero and heroine can relax enough to resolve their personal conflicts.

It's generally considered to be an especially elegant ending when all the tropes of a story can be brought to resolution in a single, cohesive climax. But the practical reality is that this is simply not always possible. Often, a story needs two or more climactic scenes, one to resolve each major trope.

Helpful Hint: The general rule is to resolve the least important trope first and the most important trope last. In a story that's primarily a romance, the trope

most likely to tear your hero and heroine apart will be the most important trope and resolved last.

If you're combining a non-romance trope with a romance trope in a romance story, the romance trope will still usually resolve last.

Vice versa, in a non-romance story, all else being equal, the romance would resolve first and the major trope of the primary story would resolve last.

I stated earlier that I arbitrarily divided my master list of universal romance tropes into four categories: Internal Tropes, External Tropes, Backstory Tropes, and Hook Tropes.

In point of fact, however, each of these categories of tropes is a bit different from the others, and the tropes in each of these categories lean into one specific aspect of story more than the other aspects.

The internal tropes lean into the thoughts, feelings, and emotions of the hero and heroine. The external tropes emphasize the world the hero and heroine live in. The backstory trope focuses on past events in the hero and heroine's lives, and the hook trope focuses on how they meet.

A possible, and entirely plausible, way to layer tropes to form a complex and layered love story would be to choose one trope from each of these categories (which is to say, one trope from each of the four books in this series) and combine the four into a single story.

By choosing from these different categories, the tropes will generally tend not to compete against one another too violently for the characters', and hence the reader's or viewer's, attention. This is because each trope focuses on a conflict that pertains to a separate part of each character's personality, environment, past, and current situation.

Of course, you could also choose two tropes from one category and one trope from another category. Or one trope from each of three of the categories. Or four tropes from one category. And so on, and so on.

The number of possible combinations of tropes is astronomical. (For my fellow math nerds out there, there are over 8,500,000 possible combinations of tropes in my master list of 130 or so universal romance tropes.)

Another way to pick tropes would be to assign one to your hero and another to your heroine. In this case, you can pick complimentary tropes that work well together, or you can choose tropes that work strongly against each other.

Years ago, a literary agent told me about a demographic study my publisher had done that showed readers who liked books about sheikhs and kidnapped harem girls also tended to like stories about arranged marriages and artificial insemination babies. (I swear, I'm not making that up.) The publisher was looking for a story that combined all three tropes. The agent had an author client who struggled for months to come up with a story that included all three of those elements but had failed.

Tropoholic that I am, I took it as a personal challenge to come up with exactly that story. While I did end up substituting an adjacent trope—a secret pregnancy for the artificial insemination, I found I really enjoyed the challenge of combining several wildly unrelated tropes.

The book resulting from that exercise ended up winning several prestigious fiction awards and garnered many glowing reviews that inevitably mentioned how fresh, different, and exciting the story's twists and turns were.

It's also worth mentioning that, as the print publishing industry moves toward more online sales and away from rigid divisions of print fiction genres (historically driven by booksellers' need to know where in the store to shelve books), crossover fiction combining non-romance story elements with romantic story elements is becoming more and more common.

Romance writers are borrowing tropes from many other genres of fiction to enrich and broaden the types of stories they can tell. At the same time, many writers of other genres of fiction now feel free to pull romance tropes into their stories.

Likewise, with the advent of streaming television networks' willingness to experiment, and the sheer number of shows going into production, opportunity abounds to play with genre mash-up stories, layering multiple tropes in one project, and interesting or unexpected mixtures of tropes.

The bottom line: the number of possible combinations of universal romance tropes, genre-specific romance tropes, and tropes from other genres of storytelling is nearly endless, which is why it's still possible to write fresh, new, exciting stories out of the same tropes that every storyteller in history has used.

That said, let's dive into the tropes themselves...

4

ACCIDENTAL PREGNANCY

DEFINITION

Obviously, in this trope the heroine gets pregnant unexpectedly, and fallout from this event ensues. The existence of a child may be the catalyst that draws the hero and heroine together into a long-term relationship, or a child may threaten the survival of an existing relationship.

This is the quintessential secret that cannot be kept indefinitely. It *is* going to be revealed, and the consequences *will* follow. While this could technically be classed simply as a dangerous secret trope, it's such a common story type and has such enormous consequences —the creation of a human life—that it qualifies to be described as a trope unto itself.

This trope is amenable to a wide range of emotional tones. They will be determined largely by the kind of relationship the mother and father had before the pregnancy happened and by how the two of them relate to the idea of becoming parents after the pregnancy is revealed. This can be anything from a comic trope, to a suspenseful one, or even a deeply tragic story.

This is also a fairly common secondary trope in a story that layers several tropes on top of one another. When this story arc isn't carrying the full weight of the story by itself, the range of emotional tones that can be struck around an accidental pregnancy becomes even broader. The prospect of becoming a parent can provoke complex, nuanced, and sometimes very painful reactions in human beings

In the case of a romance where a happily ever after ending, or some variation thereof, is guaranteed, the hero and heroine usually resolve this trope by being together in love and committed to raising this child together.

The core of this trope is a mistake, which will ultimately require forgiveness or redemption, or both, and the core is a dangerous secret ... perhaps the most dangerous secret most people will ever keep.

ADJACENT TROPES
--Dangerous Secret
--Baby on the Doorstep
--Secret Baby

WHY READERS/VIEWERS LOVE THIS TROPE
-- the secret wish for a baby
--the baby as a great gift received
--forgiveness for one's mistakes
--the father, aka knight in shining armor, as rescuer of the mother, aka damsel in distress
--having a family of your own
--historically great fertility is of great value, and this may linger among some audience members

OBLIGATORY SCENES
THE BEGINNING:
The accidental pregnancy is revealed. Obviously, it's revealed to

the now expectant mother, and it's also revealed to the reader. It may or may not be revealed immediately to the father.

The beginning may include the hero and heroine having sex, typically unplanned sex or sex where an accident occurs.

The beginning of the story will establish the type of relationship the mother and father have prior to the pregnancy happening, how casual or serious it is, and what they think of each other. Often their attitudes about parenthood and family will also be established up front since this is likely to be a major source of conflict throughout the story.

Also, the beginning may include the heroine discovering she's pregnant. But the only obligatory scene absolutely necessary to get this trope rolling is that the accidental pregnancy is established as a problem.

THE MIDDLE:

The fallout from this pregnancy commences.

The fact that this pregnancy is a problem to either or both mother and father of the baby becomes clear. That problem starts, well, causing problems. If it were simply a matter of mom-to-be and dad-to-be already being in love, delighted to have a baby, and deciding to get married or form some sort of permanent partnership, there wouldn't be any conflict whatsoever to resolve, and hence no story to tell.

The hero and heroine may or may not reveal the pregnancy to others. This may be a source of major external conflict for the hero and heroine to resolve over the course of the story.

The various choices in how to deal with the accidental pregnancy are laid out. These choices may pose internal or external conflicts to the parents-to-be. Some tough decisions are going to have to get made by the end of the story, but the middle of the story is where we'll see the hero and heroine wrestling with those choices.

Conflict ensues over what the hero and heroine should do about this child.

Conflict may also ensue over how the accident happened. Blame may fly between hero, heroine, and possibly between secondary characters and the hero/heroine.

Whatever tone you've set for the relationship between these characters in the beginning will intensify in the middle. A funny story will get funnier. A messy story will get messier. A dark story will get much darker.

BLACK MOMENT:

The hero and heroine cannot agree on how to respond to the forthcoming baby, and it appears they will not be able to come together to raise this child. At all.

The hero and/or heroine cannot forgive the other for this accident happening.

There is no chance a family will emerge from this mess.

THE END:

The pregnancy and baby to come are accepted by both partners, who have forgiven each other, and are now in love and committed to being parents together.

The external and internal conflicts revolving around this pregnancy and its fallout have largely been resolved. This trope may not have a perfect outcome—because what family is perfect after all—but the reader and the main characters at least see a way forward that's safe and happy for everyone including the baby.

Often, we see the baby, now welcome and loved. Baby, mommy, and daddy are a happy family.

KEY SCENES

--the moment of discovering the pregnancy
--revealing the pregnancy to the father

--the father's reaction

--other peoples' reactions

THINGS TO THINK ABOUT WHEN WRITING THIS TROPE

First and foremost, how did this pregnancy occur? The circumstances of the baby's conception will set the tone for the entire rest of the story.

- Was it a one-night stand?
- A casual or drunken pickup?
- A case of mistaken identity (which is another trope in its own right)?
- An accident within an established relationship?
- An intentional act of deception by one parent?

Were measures taken by one or both to prevent an unplanned pregnancy? If so, what measures? Why did they fail?

When did the sex that led to the pregnancy happen—before or after the story begins? Are you going to show this to the reader or not?

When does the heroine find out she's pregnant? Before or after the story begins? How will the heroine figure out she's pregnant? How does she react to the news?

Was this pregnancy genuinely accidental? We could also phrase this question as, is it possible this pregnancy was consciously not accidental or unconsciously not accidental? It's a good bet that one parent or the other will ask this question of his or her partner at some point in the story.

How will the hero react to the news? This, too, will set much of the book's tone.

How well do the hero and heroine know each other before the

pregnancy occurs? How much better will they get to know each other over the course of the story? Do they have similar ideas on how to parent? On how a family should look and live? Or is this going to be a major source of conflict for them? How to raise your children is one of those really deep, core beliefs most people hold. Beware of creating a mom-to-be and dad-to-be with such different ideas about parenting that they will never plausibly agree on how to raise the baby. People whose core beliefs are fundamentally at odds rarely end up happy together for the long term, and readers/viewers know this.

What problems are caused by this pregnancy?

What external forces make this pregnancy a tremendous problem?

Who needs to forgive whom in this story?

How will the hero and heroine acknowledge this momentous accident and its long-term consequences that will utterly change their lives?

TROPE TRAPS

The hero or heroine was TSTL (Too Stupid to Live) in conceiving this child. In general, being TSTL makes the hero and/or heroine unappealing, unsympathetic, and unlikable to readers or viewers.

One of the parents intentionally caused this pregnancy and comes across as dishonest or deceptive to readers/viewers and hence, is completely unheroic and unsympathetic. If you're going to do this in your story, you must create a strong enough reason for the character deceiving his or her lover that the reader will forgive them for it.

Hero fails to engage with the baby and to embrace becoming a father.

Hero fails to offer genuine emotional support to the heroine.

Hero or heroine fails to take responsibility for his/her part in the accidental pregnancy happening.

Heroine remains ambivalent about being a parent and doesn't

fully step up to taking care of the unborn baby or herself or may even do things that could possibly harm the child.

The hero and heroine have diametrically opposed ideas on parenting that they will never be able to settle. Readers and viewers know this will set up intractable problems in the relationship and family that can likely never be overcome. Which is to say, whatever temporary happily ever after you craft won't be believable as a long-term HEA.

ACCIDENTAL PREGNANCY TROPE IN ACTION
Movies:

- *Knocked Up*
- *17 Again*
- *Saved!*
- *Fools Rush In*

Books:

- *Never Too Far* by Abby Glines
- *Effortless* by S.C. Stevens
- *Mine* by Katy Evans
- *Knight* by Kristin Ashley
- *Come Away With Me* by Kristen Proby
- *Reaper's Property* by Joanna Wilde
- *Something Blue* by Emily Griffin
- *The Duke and I* by Julia Quinn
- *Sweet Evil* by Wendy Higgins

5

AMNESIA

DEFINITION

Before we define this trope a short lesson in neurology, or more accurately, amnesia myths, is in order.

Retrograde amnesia is a form of amnesia where the victim loses memory of the past and is, in fact, extremely rare. In these cases, the victim typically emerges from a coma and loses not only their memory, but also the ability to speak or form sentences, and suffers serious cognitive deficits including difficulties in perception and learning.

Much more common is anterograde amnesia where the victim loses the ability to retain new information. A victim can meet the same person over and over, believing they've never met before, or this victim might read the same magazine over and over, never realizing they've read it many times.

Generalized amnesia, where the victim forgets their identity and all details of their previous life but retains the ability to act and speak normally, is exceedingly rare, and many psychologists contend that it doesn't exist. When victims do exhibit generalized amnesia, the source is typically not a head injury but rather some sort of psychological trauma or extreme stress.

Last but not least on the hit parade of false amnesia myths is the notion that another blow to the head will cure the amnesia originally caused by a blow to the head.

All of that said, the amnesia trope remains a popular one in romance fiction. By all means, feel free to write it. Just understand that you are creating a fictional reality which must have an internally consistent set of rules about how amnesia works in your world. You will need to explain to the audience how amnesia works in your story and then you'll need to stick to that explanation.

The amnesia trope is defined as a story where a hero or heroine suffers memory loss, falls in love while discovering his or her new identity, and ultimately regains his or her memory while keeping their new love and possibly their new life.

The major conflict in this trope may arise from the problems of not knowing who oneself is, from challenges associated with beginning a new life, or with the problems of the return of the old life to disrupt the new life in progress.

At its core, this is a trope of reinvention of self, of a clean slate in life or a do-over if you will. Often it is a trope of coming to terms with past mistakes.

ADJACENT TROPES
--Fresh Start
--Running Away From Home
--Secret Identity
--Love Triangle

WHY READERS/VIEWERS LOVE THIS TROPE
--starting a whole new life
--a complete reset, a do-over on life, if you will
--being rescued when completely helpless
--being taken care of, nursed, protected from the big, bad world

--finding a new tribe that's much better than your old one

OBLIGATORY SCENES
THE BEGINNING:

The hero or heroine wakes up—literally or metaphorically—into a totally new and unfamiliar world and meets the eventual love interest.

The reader may or may not be shown how the amnesiac character came to be in this situation. For example, was the amnesiac injured or traumatized in some way?

This is where you will set up the rules of how amnesia works in your world. A doctor may explain it to the amnesiac or to the love interest, or the amnesiac may have to discover how it works for himself or herself.

You may or may not choose to give the reader a glimpse of the world the amnesiac has forgotten. Doing this may require point of view shifts to characters in the world the amnesiac has left behind, or it may require some sort of parallel story structure where we see the past world or left-behind world through flashbacks, backstory, clues discovered in the new world, or some other literary device.

THE MIDDLE:

The amnesiac hero or heroine learns to live in this strange, new world and in the process falls in love.

The amnesiac's memory probably begins to return. How this happens will depend on the rules you've set up for how amnesia works in your world and how memory returns. You may choose to have memory come back in small snippets, all at once, or some combination of the two. Again, you may choose to rely on some literary device to trigger the return of memory—reading letters or a journal, dreams, emails or texts from a stranger, or something else altogether.

The forgotten world begins to impinge on the amnesiac's new reality. This is probably a source of external conflict, but it may also be a source of internal conflict within the amnesiac or between the amnesiac and their growing love interest.

The conflict between old world and new builds toward a terrible choice—the old world without the new love or the new world with the new love.

A common device in amnesia stories is that there's a love interest left behind in the old world who reemerges and throws the amnesiac into a terrible love triangle. This dilemma will develop in the middle of the story in most cases.

BLACK MOMENT:

The amnesiac character must finally confront the terrible choices posed by his or her amnesia, and there's no good outcome to be had. Every potential choice includes a disaster to someone else.

If a love triangle has been established, the amnesiac must make a terrible choice to abandon someone he or she loves. The black moment may be the amnesiac's refusal to choose one or the other (potentially losing both of his or her loves).

The amnesiac may leave behind the new world and new love to return to their old life, abandoning the new love interest.

THE END:

The amnesiac remembers all, and probably more importantly finds a way to incorporate the new love interest and lessons from their new life into their old one. This may be a bittersweet outcome for some of the characters in the story.

The amnesiac finally finds a way to move forward into the future. This future can be a return to the old world with the new love interest, or it can be a move fully into the new world with the new love interest, retaining none or only some of the old world.

Any love triangles are resolved.

The amnesia itself is resolved according to the rules for it that you've established in your fictional world.

KEY SCENES

--H/h waking up and realizing they remember nothing
--revealing the memory loss to the love interest
--the moment when memory returns (if it does)
--the moment the past shows up (in whatever form that takes)
--the moment of decision of which world to live in going forward

THINGS TO THINK ABOUT WHEN WRITING THIS TROPE

How are you going to make this ultimately unscientific premise believable, or will you choose to forge ahead without explaining the fictitious, fantastical nature of the amnesia? (Note: The latter choice is fine as long as you commit to the premise and keep your science of how amnesia works in your book's world consistent.)

What event has caused the hero or heroine's amnesia?

How much has the amnesiac hero or heroine forgotten? Has the hero or heroine only forgotten events? Forgotten how to care for himself or herself? Forgotten how to function in the day-to-day world? (Note: Because you're in effect making up the kind of amnesia your character has, you have free rein, here. You are creating an affliction in the same way you might build a magic system in a fantasy world.)

What vital information have they forgotten that becomes a huge problem for the hero or heroine in this story?

What person(s), event(s), or revelation(s) from the amnesiac character's past will show up and blow up the new world? When will this element show up? How will they blow up the new world?

What conflicts will erupt between the old world and the new world?

How will returning memory manifest itself to the amnesiac hero or heroine? Flashbacks? Dreams? Memories triggered by sensory moments? Something else?

Does the old world inevitably suck the amnesiac back into it against the amnesiac's will, or does the amnesiac voluntarily return to their old world? If they return voluntarily, why do they do it? Out of love? Fear? Responsibility? Need to tie up loose ends to move into the new life?

How much of the amnesiac's memory will return by the end of your story?

How deeply does the love interest of the amnesiac fall into the role of caretaker?

How much of a do-over is this new life for the person who lost his or her memory?

What lessons does the amnesiac learn in their new life that he or she will take into solving the lingering problems in their old life? Vice versa, what knowledge/lessons from the old life are brought into the new one?

TROPE TRAPS

Failing to create an internally consistent memory affliction in your amnesiac character. For example, a character has forgotten how to cook, but still remembers how to shave or how to drive. Either they remember how to do daily tasks or they don't.

Not presenting a plausible return of memory, either in the pace of memory's return or failing to explain convincingly what causes the amnesiac's memory to return.

Trying to create a fictitious form of amnesia and somehow justify it medically without weaving in actual medical facts. (This is an all or nothing trope. The story either has to fully embrace the medical facts of amnesia or fully ignore them and create a fictitious version of memory loss.)

Caretaker of the amnesiac becomes more of a parental figure than a viable love interest.

The amnesiac's story completely overshadows the character arc and personal growth of the new love interest.

Unsatisfying meshing of the old world and new world as the amnesiac regains his or her memory and moves into the future.

AMNESIA TROPE IN ACTION
Movies:

- *While You Were Sleeping*
- *Finding Nemo*
- *Before I Go to Sleep*
- *Memento*
- *50 First Dates*
- *Captain Marvel*
- *The Bourne Identity*

Books:

- *What Alice Forgot* by Liana Moriarty
- *Until You* by Judith McNaught
- *The Darkest Hour* by Maya Banks
- *Heart of Obsidian* by Nalini Singh
- *Remember Me* by Sophie Kinsella
- *Dreams of a Dark Warrior* by Kresley Cole
- *The Opportunist* by Tarryn Fisher
- *Rogue Rider* by Larissa Ione
- *Kiss of the Night* by Sherrilyn Kenyon

6

ANTIHERO/ANTIHEROINE

DEFINITION

An antihero (or antiheroine) is a main character who lacks the traditional qualities associated with noble or heroic central characters. They lack ideals, morals, or positive qualities typically associated with good or heroic people. This is *not* a (secretly) good character who is simply acting badly. The antihero has no compunction and no guilt about behaving badly according to the values of society.

For this character, the ends justify the means. This is a character who does the wrong thing for the right reasons. The antihero or antiheroine is necessarily a complex character who, in a romance novel, will undergo a difficult journey of fundamental change. At its core, this is a story of massive personal transformation.

ADJACENT TROPES

--Bad Boy/Girl Reformed

--Mafia Love

--Forgiveness

--Rebellious Hero/Heroine

. . .

WHY READERS/VIEWERS LOVE THIS TROPE

--he/she loves me so much that he/she is willing to change for me

--the danger of the bad boy/girl

--getting to be bad yourself

--striking back against (something, someone) along with the antihero

--forbidden love

--(naughty or taboo) secret fantasies fulfilled

OBLIGATORY SCENES
THE BEGINNING:

The antihero/antiheroine, unapologetically "bad", is introduced. The antihero demonstrates his or her lack of heroic (or antiheroic) morals, values, and ideals. The antihero and his or her love interest are thrown together.

THE MIDDLE:

The plot middle to this story usually involves the antihero and his or her love being forced to work together toward some goal, but they disagree about how to go about attaining the goal. The character development middle of this trope involves the antihero and his or her love interest coming into great conflict over their disparate ideals, morals, opinions, and behavior choices.

BLACK MOMENT:

The antihero refuses to change for his or her love interest. The goal they've been working toward is not only unachieved but lost.

THE END:

The antihero finally changes for his or her love interest. By changing, the goal they've been working toward can finally be reached.

KEY SCENES

--realization by the love interest of how antiheroic the H/h is

--realization by H/h that they want to change

--realization by each character that he/she loves the other

--moment of antihero asking for forgiveness (if he/she asks)

--forgiveness granted by love interest for past wrongs

--forgiveness granted to self by antihero for past wrongs

THINGS TO THINK ABOUT WHEN WRITING THIS TROPE

What are your antihero/antiheroine's main negative qualities?

What form does your antihero's behavior take? Is he/she a pragmatist who only does what's necessary to get the job done? Is this character downright unscrupulous—does he or she go out of his/her way to do bad things? Or does this character simply go where others fear to tread and interact with evil so dark that no regular person would attempt it?

Why is your antihero the way he or she is? What trauma or set of circumstances turned this person into who they are today?

How will you force together your antihero and love interest? These are probably two people who would normally never choose to hang out together.

What qualities or behaviors in your antihero will make them likable, or even lovable, to your readers/viewers?

When in your story will you make your antihero likable? Do you need to do this immediately, or will you wait a bit into the story to reveal endearing qualities about him or her?

Why does your love interest continue to stick around with and for your antihero over the course of the story?

What qualities in your love interest will be irresistible to your antihero? Why are they irresistible?

Why does this love interest, specifically, get through to your antihero when no one else has before? Is it something about the love interest? Or is it the timing? Perhaps this is a particular problem they must solve together?

What do the antihero and his or her love interest have in common? What qualities and beliefs do they actually share?

What crisis will finally force the antihero to consider changing? The obvious answer to this is that he/she has fallen in love with the love interest. However, it will be a huge undertaking for any adult to make real and lasting change to their core values. It's going to take more than just love for your antihero to fundamentally transform. Something must utterly tear them apart, challenge everything they have ever believed, or cost the antihero everything they are as a human being for them to change at this deep of a level.

How is the love interest changed by the antihero's journey? Although your antihero will probably be taking the most difficult internal emotional journey in your story, the love interest's journey from (potentially) naïve innocence to a broader world view may be nearly as transformative.

TROPE TRAPS

Failing to create a likable antihero. This is first in the list of trope traps because it's the most critical trap to avoid when creating the antihero.

Waiting too long to show the reader something likable or lovable about the antihero. Romance readers and viewers expect to fall in love with the hero/heroine along with the love interest in your story. But an unlikable antihero risks alienating your reader so badly they put down the book and never pick it up again or your viewer so badly they turn the channel or walk out of the theater midmovie.

Using a clichéd good guy behavior to make the antihero likable.

In Blake Snyder's book, *Save The Cat*, Snyder suggests that writers introduce heroic main characters by showing them doing something universally likable, for example, rescuing a cat who is stuck in a tree. While Snyder's point is excellent and may be useful in crafting a likable antihero, beware of falling into clichés to paint your antihero's secret heart of gold.

So much conflict between the antihero and love interest that readers/viewers can't possibly believe they'll ever actually fall in love.

Failing to create a believable progression between the antihero and love interest of learning to like, respect, and eventually love each other.

Failing to create a believable and compelling enough reason for the antihero and/or the love interest to move away from their deeply held morals and ideals.

Let me repeat that one: Failing to create a believable and compelling enough reason for the antihero and/or the love interest to move away from their deeply held morals and ideals. You're asking a character(s) to change at the deepest level of their being, to change the absolute core of their identity. Only an existential crisis that threatens everything they are and hold dear will force either of them to take on this Herculean task.

Creating a hero and heroine who are so fundamentally unalike or who have such opposing core values that they would never plausibly form a lasting and strong relationship *after* the crisis in the story is resolved.

ANTI-HERO TROPE IN ACTION
Television:

- *Dexter*
- *The Sopranos*
- Han Solo in *Star Wars*
- Walter White in *Breaking Bad*

. . .

Books:

- *Gone With the Wind* by Margaret Mitchell
- *The Girl With the Dragon Tattoo* by Stieg Larrson
- *Wuthering Heights* by Emily Bronte
- *A Court of Mist and Fury* by Sarah J. Maas
- *Devil in Winter* by Lisa Kleypas
- *Lothaire* by Kresley Cole

7

BAD BOY/BAD GIRL REFORMED

DEFINITION

The hero or heroine of the story starts out "bad" in some way, and the power of finding true love reforms his or her errant ways. Unlike the antihero, this character still has a fundamentally good set of morals, values, and ideals. They know they are acting against those core values and are choosing to act badly.

The core of this story is personal transformation. The bad character changes at a fundamental level into a good, or at least lovable and stable, person who is capable of sustaining a permanent, loving relationship. Typically, the other love interest is portrayed as "good" or at least a less bad foil to the bad boy/bad girl character.

It's worth pointing out that the dark and dangerous hero or heroine is not a trope in and of themselves. That's a character theme. What differentiates this trope from a tattooed, leather-jacketed biker dude as a character type is the *change* of that character into someone else. It's entirely possible to include bad boys/bad girls in a love story without ever changing them one bit. For that matter, it's entirely possible that the love interest who changes is the "good" boy or girl who goes dark/dangerous/bad. For example, Sandy in *Grease*.

At its core, this is an opposites attract story. However, it's such a common version of that larger trope that it requires description of its own.

ADJACENT TROPES
--Rebellious Hero/Heroine
--Grumpy/Sunshine
--Redemption
--Forgiveness

WHY READERS/VIEWERS LOVE THIS TROPE
--being loved so much another person will change for you
--the fantasy of a smoking hot lover
--getting to be a bad boy/bad girl, yourself
--getting away with being naughty without being caught
--just how dirty is the sex going to be?

OBLIGATORY SCENES
THE BEGINNING:
The hero or heroine is established to be bad. Typically, the other main character in the relationship is established to be not bad. A relationship between the hero and heroine commences.

THE MIDDLE:
The badness of the hero or heroine causes conflict and obstacles to the development of a stable, loving, permanent relationship.

The bad character's reform commences, typically because of the good character.

. . .

BLACK MOMENT:

The hero or heroine rejects becoming a good, or at least better, person and may also reject the relationship their partner is offering. The bad character returns to his or her bad ways. The good character cannot accept the bad boy/bad girl as is.

THE END:

The bad hero or heroine is fully reformed and embraces his or her new life and new self. Now that the bad character is fully reformed, a happily ever after is possible and finally achieved.

KEY SCENES

--demonstration to "good" love interest of how bad the bad boy/girl is

--moment when good love interest succumbs to being bad, too.

--moment when bad boy/girl reconsiders his or her life choices

--moment of decision to change by bad boy/girl

THINGS TO THINK ABOUT WHEN WRITING THIS TROPE

In what way is the hero or heroine bad? By whose standards is he or she bad? By their own standards? By the other main character's standards? By society's standards?

Is one of them reluctant to enter into this relationship? If so, why?

How and why are these two disparate people drawn to each other?

The hero and heroine aren't necessarily opposites in temperament, but they obviously have a disconnect in values or behavior. What exactly is that disconnect?

What makes the bad character irresistible?

What does the bad character represent in the life of the good character? A rebellion, escape, revenge, cure for boredom, or simply a project, for example.

What makes the bad character willing to change their ways? Why now? Why with this good person?

What makes the bad character willing to change—to really change, way down deep in their core as a person? NOTE: Making a fundamental change in values or core beliefs is very difficult and typically takes a severe emotional shock or deep trauma to accomplish. Even making a long-lasting change in behavior is a huge challenge for most people.

How does the good character push, cajole, trick, argue, coax, coerce, or otherwise get the bad character to reform? What flavor will that effort by the good character take?

In what way is the good character more like the bad character than they'd like to admit? Which is to say, how is the good character a little bit bad? How does he or she demonstrate it in the story?

How is the bad character a little bit good? How does he or she demonstrate it in the story?

What shared core values do the hero and heroine share that will make a long-term relationship possible?

What does the fully reformed bad boy/bad girl look like in the end? How far have they come in their journey of transformation?

How does the bad boy/bad girl change the good character?

What pieces of their old selves will each character retain?

TROPE TRAPS

Making value judgments about badness and goodness in characters that may be offensive to readers or viewers.

Failing to create a traumatic enough event or strong enough rationale for the bad character to change their behavior permanently.

Creating a character that's so bad he or she is not likable to readers or viewers.

Creating one-dimensionally "bad" or "good" characters that come across as cardboard caricatures of real people.

Giving the bad and good characters nothing in common that would plausibly attract them to each other.

Failing to give the bad and good characters any (or enough) shared core values upon which to build a long-term relationship.

The bad character and good character are so different that they wouldn't plausibly be compatible in the long term. Passion in the short term is all well and good, but it takes much more than that to form a deep and lasting bond.

Hero and/or heroine only seeing the other as an object rather than a person—an object of rebellion, revenge, salvation, or escape, for example.

BAD BOY/BAD GIRL REFORMED TROPE IN ACTION
Movies:

- *Grease*
- *Dirty Dancing*
- *She's All That*
- *The Girl Next Door*
- *Crazy, Stupid Love*
- *10 Things I Hate About You*

Books:

- *Lover Awakened* by J.R. Ward (really, any of the Black Dagger Brotherhood series)
- *Beautiful Disaster* by Jamie McGuire
- *Bared to You* by Sylvia Day
- *City of Bones* by Cassandra Clare

- *Hush, Hush* by Becca Fitzpatrick
- *Dead Until Dark* by Charlaine Harris
- *Never Judge a Lady by Her Cover* by Sarah Maclean
- *Ain't She Sweet* by Susan Elizabeth Phillips

8

BEAUTY AND THE BEAST

DEFINITION

This is an opposites attract trope, but so commonly used that it requires its own definition. In this trope a beautiful or civilized person falls in love with an ugly or wild and bestial person. The beautiful/civilized person tames the wild beast, thereby revealing the beautiful/civilized person trapped inside the angry, sad, possibly mean, beast.

The generous love of the beauty changes the beast into a prince charming, of course. Only then is the beast worthy of love, and only then can the beautiful person fall in love with the tamed beast and the two of them achieve happily ever after.

In the original fairy tale, the civilized beauty enters the sumptuous lair of the beast as a captive and tames the beast from within his or her own home. This may or may not be literally or figuratively included in your story.

This trope differs from the bad boy/girl reformed trope in that the reform goes a step further and requires actual destruction of the beast within a person—a much taller order than merely convincing someone to reform their bad behavior.

This is an archetypal story of how the healing power of love conquers the demons within us all.

ADJACENT TROPES
--Secret Identity
--Rags to Riches
--Hero/Heroine in Hiding

WHY READERS/VIEWERS LOVE THIS TROPE
--transforming someone with the power of your love for them

--the beast, who could have taken anyone, chose you

--there's something special about you that only one person saw

--the fantasy of being swept away from your boring or difficult life to a magical, new world

--being captive ... and additionally, taming one's captor

--utter surrender to your lover and of your lover to you

--let's be real—lots of people fantasize about having sex with a beast

OBLIGATORY SCENES
THE BEGINNING:
The frightening beast and humble but good, love interest meet. Attraction ensues, especially from the beast toward the love interest. The beauty is appalled and possibly fascinated by the beast. If following the traditional story, the beast kidnaps the beauty.

THE MIDDLE:
The beauty may resist his or her captivity but gradually comes to accept it.

The beast falls in love but is unable to express it to the beauty.

Meanwhile, the beauty glimpses hints of the kind and good person trapped inside the beast. It's a game of advance and retreat, a hint of good followed by a healthy dose of beast.

The beauty commences taming the beast, bit by bit.

BLACK MOMENT:

The beast reverts one last time to full beast behavior, frightening or disillusioning the beauty. Likewise, the beauty appears to abandon the beast and revoke his or her love for the beast. Both Beauty and Beast are devastated.

THE END:

The beast within is defeated once and for all. His or her transformation into a good person is complete. The beauty can fully—and safely—embrace the now good person with no fear of the beast returning. Happily ever after is now possible with both Beauty and Beast fully in love with each other.

KEY SCENES

--the moment of capture by the beast
--Beauty's fear of the beast revealed
--the beast's revulsion of self is revealed
--attraction sparks between these opposites
--a great sacrifice by each of them
--the moment of transformation from Beast to Man.

THINGS TO THINK ABOUT WHEN WRITING THIS TROPE

What turned a good person into a beast? What's the source of their devastating emotional wound?

What about the good and civilized beauty is irresistible to the beast besides the fact that he or she is good, kind, and civilized?

What about the sad, angry, lashing out beast is attractive to the beauty? [NOTE: Be very careful with this answer...see the trope traps below.]

How much self-loathing does your beast experience and how does your beast experience and express that self-loathing?

How much danger is the beauty in when the beast is in full beast mode?

How hard will the beast fight letting the beauty see his or her emotional wounds? What form will that fight take?

Why is the beauty determined to tame the beast, above and beyond earning his or her freedom to go home?

Why MUST the beast hold the beauty captive, or at least keep the beauty captive emotionally in a relationship with him or her?

Why doesn't the beast walk away from the beauty if he/she truly loves the beauty? Why inflict his or her emotional wounds on the beauty, knowing it will potentially cause him or her to harm the beauty?

How does the beauty stop the beast from retreating, either physically or emotionally from him or her?

How will the beast reveal his or her wounds to the beauty? How will the beauty react to that?

What form will the complete emotional and physical surrender of the beast to the beauty take?

What significant, life-changing event will occur to actually cause the beast to transform, keeping in mind that nothing short of something earth-shattering will cause any person to make such a radical transformation? How does the beauty cause or at least trigger this life-changing event?

What will their post-beast relationship look like?

How will the beauty know for sure the beast is truly vanquished forever? For that matter, how will the beast know?

. . .

TROPE TRAPS

ABUSE. Particularly if you choose to go the traditional captivity route with this trope, failing to explain why the beast MUST hold the beauty captive. Failing to overcome how creepy and stalkerish it is that the beast actually kidnaps and holds the beauty prisoner.

Stockholm Syndrome in the beauty. This is a psychological syndrome in which a person being held captive begins to identify with and grow sympathetic to his or her captor, and simultaneously becomes unsympathetic toward authorities or police. It's generally temporary. As soon as the prisoner escapes the captor, the artificial sympathy evaporates, leaving the former prisoner disillusioned, angry, and humiliated ... not a great recipe for a happily ever after between captor and prisoner.

The beauty appearing self-destructive and self-harm prone by being attracted to an individual who lashes out at him or her.

The beast appearing selfish and irresponsible by not removing his or her wounded, angry self from the object of his or her love.

Failure to explain why, if the beast truly loves the beauty, he or she sticks around to potentially hurt that person.

Failure to explain why the beauty sticks around long enough to get around to the beast's full transformation.

Failure to explain why these two people are attracted to each other, need each other, and find their soul mate in each other.

BEAUTY AND THE BEAST TROPE IN ACTION
Movies:

- *Beauty and the Beast* (duh)
- *Beauty and the Beast* TV shows (1987-1990 and 2012-2016)
- *Beautician and the Beast*
- *Blood of Beasts*
- *Beastly*

- *Phantom of the Opera*

Books:

- *Wicked Abyss* by Kresley Cole
- *The Beast* of Beswick by Amalie Howard
- *To Beguile a Beast* by Elizabeth Hoyt
- *Ravished* by Amanda Quick
- *A Curse so Dark and Lonely* by Brigid Kemmerer
- *When Beauty Tamed the Beast* by Eloisa James

9

BURDENED BY BEAUTY (OR TALENT)

DEFINITION

The hero or heroine in this story is so physically attractive that others fail to see the person beneath. The burdened by beauty hero or heroine feels unseen, unknown, and unloved for anything other than their looks. This character craves deep and meaningful interaction with a love interest who sees them for who they really are beneath the outward appearance.

In a less literal interpretation, this trope is about a character who is burdened by extreme talent, perhaps making beautiful art, music, prose. For whatever reason, this character is idolized for that thing of beauty that they do or create. Like the physically beautiful hero/heroine, this character feels unseen and unknown behind their immense talent that all the world sees and loves.

Both of these characters may have dark secrets or an inner world that stands in sharp contrast to the beautiful or talented exterior they show the world.

At his or her core, the hero-heroine burdened by beauty or talent is a lonely, unknown soul desperate to reveal their true self and find deep, meaningful, and fulfilling love. This character's journey is one of revealing their true self, reconciling outer light with inner darkness, and filling the hole in their heart.

ADJACENT TROPES
--Nerd/Geek/Genius
--Socially Awkward
--Secret Identity

WHY READERS/VIEWERS LOVE THIS TROPE
--who doesn't want to be extremely beautiful or talented?
--being truly loved exactly as you are
--finding one's soulmate
--not being alone anymore
--being the only person to whom someone reveals their innermost secrets, being in on the secret no one else knows
--sharing your beautiful/talented mate's fame and fortune

OBLIGATORY SCENES
THE BEGINNING:
The physical beauty or talent of the hero/heroine is established, along with the character's conflicted relationship with his/her personal attributes. The love interest may or may not be dazzled by the hero/heroine's appearance or talent.

THE MIDDLE:
The love interest is attracted to the beautiful or talented hero/heroine, but the beautiful hero/heroine does not trust the sincerity or legitimacy of that attraction.

The inner life or secret(s) of the burdened hero/heroine are revealed, for better or worse, to the love interest.

Conflict ensues as the beautiful hero/heroine refuses to commit to the relationship or believe the feelings the love interest expresses. The love interest fights an uphill battle to prove that his or her feelings are real.

BLACK MOMENT:

The worst secret of the burdened character is revealed, and the love interest recoils.

OR

The beautiful or talented hero/heroine ultimately rejects the love interest's grand expression of true love.

THE END:

The love interest finally proves once and for all that he/she loves the beautiful hero/heroine regardless of how they look, what they've done, what their secret is, or how broken they seem. The beautiful hero/heroine finally accepts the true love of their soulmate.

KEY SCENES

--the first time the love interest sees the beautiful/talented hero or heroine

--the moment they meet

--revelation by beautiful/talented hero or heroine that they resent or hate their attribute

--moment when beautiful/talented hero or heroine first feels truly seen

--moment when beautiful/talented hero or heroine first feels loved for themselves

. . .

THINGS TO THINK ABOUT WHEN WRITING THIS TROPE

How will you make the beautiful/talented character likable to readers or viewers? What are this character's flaws and human failings that make them relatable?

Does this character have a dark secret or ugly inner world that stands in sharp contrast to their exterior beauty or talent?

How does the beautiful or talented hero/heroine perceive himself/herself? Do they see themselves as beautiful and talented or do they only see their own shortcomings?

Does the beautiful/talented hero/heroine feel like a fraud or not? Why?

How confident is the hero/heroine in his or her beauty or talent? Why or why not?

How have people around the beautiful hero/heroine reacted to them in the past, and how has that shaped this character?

Were they child prodigies or did the beauty/talent manifest later?

What benefits and burdens does this character live with as a result of their beauty or talent? How do these benefits affect this character for better and worse? How does it affect how they live their life?

How does being around the beautiful/talented character affect the love interest? Does it make them insecure? Feel bad about themselves? Uplift them? Inspire them?

How does the beautiful/talented person's isolation, loneliness and/or poor sense of self-worth or self-esteem manifest? Do they lash out? Are they self-destructive? Withdrawn? Reclusive?

How does the love interest see past the dazzling exterior of the beautiful/talented person? What do they see when they finally get past the exterior? Is the inner person a child or an adult?

How does the love interest heal the beautiful/talented person?

What does the love interest get out of loving this person? How does this relationship fulfill the love interest?

. . .

TROPE TRAPS

Failing to create a likable beautiful/talented hero or heroine. Creating a character that your audience resents, is jealous of, or whom your audience thinks doesn't deserve their special gift(s).

Creating a superficial hero-heroine who is not a complex, fully realized human being behind their beauty or talent. Failing to create a contrasting inner landscape for this character.

Painting the love interest as nothing but a self-sacrificing care-taker who parents the inner child of the beautiful/talented character, setting up a deeply unequal and unhealthy relationship dynamic.

Failing to uncover an adult (capable of returning their partner's love) beneath the special attributes of the burdened hero/heroine. Wounded or petulant children don't make for good romance heroes or heroines.

Creating a deeply unequal relationship where one partner does most of the taking and the other does most of the giving.

Creating too perfect a character—too beautiful, too talented, too nice, too self-aware, too mature. At some point, characters cease to be believable.

Failing to give the 'average' love interest their own problems or hang-ups to overcome or giving them too many imperfections to real-istically overcome.

Not creating compelling positive qualities in the love interest that would realistically attract the beautiful/talented character to them.

BURDENED BY BEAUTY (OR TALENT) TROPE IN ACTION
Movies

- *Amadeus*
- *Miss Congeniality*
- *The Devil Wears Prada*
- *Harry Potter* movies

. . .

Books

- *It Had To Be You* by Susan Elizabeth Phillips
- *Saving Grace* by Julie Garwood
- *Romancing Mr. Bridgerton* by Julia Quinn
- *Pretty Face* by Lucy Parker
- *Dukes Prefer Blondes* by Loretta Chase

10
CELIBATE HERO/HEROINE

DEFINITION

As the name implies, the hero/heroine in this trope chooses not to have sex, ever. This can be an only before truly being in love decision, an only before marriage choice, or an after-marriage condition of the relationship. This is not a character who just isn't interested in sex. The celibate character knows exactly what they're giving up but chooses to sacrifice sex anyway.

In the past, it was the norm for heroines in fiction to make this choice, or to have this choice made for them, so much so that it hardly registered as a trope. Indeed, in certain genres of romance, the celibate-before-marriage heroine is still common. That said, in much of romance today, women who have sex before marriage are so common and widely accepted that we can now expand this trope to include celibate heroines as a specific trope. In both the case of the celibate hero and heroine, being celibate is an obstacle to love that must be overcome.

This is one of those tropes where the shorthand name of it implies a character trait, rather than a full trope. An actual descriptive name of this trope would be something like, Celibate Hero/Heroine Gives Up Their Celibacy for Love.

. . .

ADJACENT TROPES
--Virgin Hero/Heroine
--Oblivious to Love
--First Love
--Secret identity
--Straight Arrow Seduced

WHY READERS/VIEWERS LOVE THIS TROPE
--he/she waited just for me
--I'll be the only person he/she ever loves
--purity is appealing
--shaping/teaching a lover to be perfect for you
--I'm so sexy/attractive that he/she can't resist me

OBLIGATORY SCENES
THE BEGINNING:

This type of hero or heroine begins the story operating under a vow of celibacy. The reason for this vow is established. The potential love interest's problem with this vow is also established.

A situation, or someone, challenges the celibate character's commitment to their vow.

THE MIDDLE:

The celibate hero or heroine is thrown into situations whose likely outcome is sex. Their commitment waivers, but they stand their ground. The love interest may be intentionally or unintentionally tempting the celibate character.

The middle of this type of story will be a continuous chain of temptations to the celibate character, whose commitment to their vow will be sorely tested.

BLACK MOMENT:

The celibate character gives in to temptation and has sex with their love interest.

OR

The love interest has had it with the celibate character's stubborn insistence on celibacy and gives up on the relationship.

THE END:

The celibate character is finally able to release themselves from their vow because the conditions under which they must stay celibate have changed (for example, the hero and heroine have gotten married). The hero and heroine finally consummate their relationship, and in so doing, their love is complete and happily ever after is now possible.

KEY SCENES

--when the noncelibate character finds out the other main character is celibate

--temptation scenes where the hero/heroine gets closer and closer to breaking the celibate character's vow

--judgment by an outside character of the now non-celibate character who broke their vow of celibacy

--establishment of a new set of values for the previously celibate character

THINGS TO THINK ABOUT WHEN WRITING THIS TROPE

Why is the celibate hero or heroine celibate? Is this an externally imposed vow or something they've decided for themselves? Does something specific have to happen before the celibate character can have sex, and if so, what's that event?

How celibate is your character? Which is to say, is sex icky to them, or is it something they crave but choose to deny themselves?

What truly compelling reason does the celibate hero or heroine have to break his or her vow? Or will they complete the conditions of their vow and be able to end their celibacy in good conscience?

Is the celibate person's vow not to have sex based in a personal emotional reason or something else?

Is the reason for their celibacy secret or not?

How will the love interest feel about and react to the hero or heroine's vow of celibacy?

What sorts of problems will the hero or heroine's celibacy introduce into the relationship?

What tactics will the other partner employ to convince the celibate character to have sex?

Will the celibate character resent the love interest's ploys to get them to have sex or be grateful for them?

What are the stakes if the celibate hero/heroine never has sex? What will be lost? What will be gained?

What is the would-be romantic partner's motivation to hang in there until the celibate hero or heroine sorts out whether or not to do the deed?

After finally making love, does the formerly celibate character renew his or her celibacy vow or not? If not, does he or she cast aside other old values or beliefs as well?

Is giving in and finally having sex a defeat or a victory for the celibate character? How does the answer to this question affect the final outcome of the relationship?

TROPE TRAPS

On the assumption that most people enjoy sex—a lot—it will take a serious set of circumstances to make your celibate hero/heroine completely swear off sex forever, or at least until a specific set of circumstances is met. The trap, here, is creating a flimsy excuse for a character taking their celibacy oath.

Creating a celibate character with such a rigid set of morals that they're unlikable to readers/viewers.

Creating a love interest that comes across as an evil temptress/tempter or who is only out to debauch the pure, celibate character.

Creating a love interest that is more villain than worthy partner of the celibate character.

Creating a celibate character who comes across as a villain for withholding the physical intimacy their partner deserves, craves, or needs from them.

Once the celibate hero/heroine gives in and has sex, they end up looking insincere about their vow and just pretending to be genuinely celibate.

Celibate hero/heroine looks weak for giving in to temptation.

Creating a love interest without a compelling reason to stick around for the celibate character to get past their block to having sex.

CELIBATE HERO TROPE IN ACTION
Movies:

- *The 40-Year-Old Virgin*
- *The Golden Child*
- *Unforgiven*
- *Dragnet*
- *Star Wars: Attack of the Clones*
- *Impromptu*

Books:

- *Twilight* by Stephanie Meyers
- *The Obsidian Trilogy* by Mercedes Lackey
- *Sheepherder's Daughter* by Elizabeth Moon
- *Lover Enshrined* by J.R. Ward
- *Magic Bites* by Ilona Andrews

11

CLUMSY/BUMBLING/THOUGHTLESS HERO/HEROINE

DEFINITION

One of the main characters is, as the title implies, clumsy, bumbles his/her way through life, or is just thoughtless. This is the character who always manages to say or do the wrong thing at the wrong moment. This trope could certainly also be a simple character theme. However, in the trope, this character ultimately overcomes their goofball tendencies to find true love, and in fact, their clumsiness may be exactly the thing that ends up landing them the love of their life. This is a trope of personal transformation from bumbler to plausible romantic love interest.

ADJACENT TROPES

--Nerd/Geek/Genius
--Socially Awkward
--Oblivious to Love

WHY READERS/VIEWERS LOVE THIS TROPE

--we all feel clumsy, thoughtless, or out of place sometimes

--someone loves us enough to humiliate themselves to have us

--I fixed you

OBLIGATORY SCENES
THE BEGINNING:

The clumsiness, bumbling actions, or thoughtlessness of the main character is demonstrated. This trait either causes a major problem for the potential love interest, embarrasses the potential love interest, or absolutely drives the love interest crazy. True love between the clumsy hero/heroine and their love interest seems impossible.

THE MIDDLE:

The bumbling hero/heroine makes their best effort to woo the skeptical potential love interest. Things go from bad to worse, to terrible.

We could describe the entire middle with the simple phrase: shenanigans ensue.

Although this is frequently a comic trope at its core, this can also be a completely serious trope, where the clumsy character's timing is epically bad, and they keep making a bad situation even worse.

BLACK MOMENT:

The main character's clumsiness, bumbling, or thoughtlessness ruins everything, and there is no way to come back from the mess they've made. The love interest is done putting up with the bumbling hero who has finally, (unwittingly) gone too far in hurting them.

THE END:

The bumbling hero or heroine makes a grand gesture of apology or finally succeeds at pulling off a redeeming action without messing it up. The love interest forgives the bumbler and confesses their true love of the endearing hot mess who is the clumsy character.

KEY SCENES

--the love interest finds the bumbling/thoughtless character adorable

--the bumbling character breaks or ruins something really important to the love interest

--love interest privately or to the main character expresses their hurt or anger over the ongoing accidents/thoughtlessness

--bumbling/thoughtless character feels remorse

THINGS TO THINK ABOUT WHEN WRITING THIS TROPE

What form will the clumsy hero/heroine's behavior take? Do they say or do the wrong thing? Not know the social conventions? Try their best but always come up short? Just have the worst luck ever?

What makes the bumbler likable to readers/viewers?

What event(s) in your story absolutely have to go right? And of course, how will the bumbler royally mess them up?

Will the potential love interest be embarrassed by the bumbler? Humiliated by them? How does the potential love interest react to this?

How and when will the love interest forgive the bumbler for their faux pas?

How, when, and why will the bumbler finally stop constantly doing/saying the wrong thing and start to get things right? I mean, who wants to live their entire life around someone who is forever sticking their foot in their mouth, knocking things over, or spilling drinks down your front?

. . .

TROPE TRAPS

Making the bumbler too annoying for readers or viewers to like.

Creating a clumsy hero who is so frustrating to readers that they throw your book against a wall or viewers stop watching your show or movie.

Creating a TSTL bumbling hero/heroine (Too Stupid To Live)

Making the accidents and mishaps so frequent and disastrous that they become utterly unbelievable.

Creating a completely unbelievable attraction between two people who are so dissimilar that they have nothing at all in common upon which to build a relationship, let alone love.

Humiliating the love interest until you make readers/viewers feel uncomfortable.

Creating a love interest with such low self-esteem that they allow themselves to be embarrassed, humiliated, and hurt by the bumbler's constant mistakes and missteps, hence readers/viewers don't relate to or like the character.

Magically fixing the bumbler's tendency to make mistakes or say/do the wrong thing.

CLUMSY/BUMBLING/THOUGHTLESS HERO/HEROINE TROPE IN ACTION
Movies:

- *Pink Panther*
- *Notting Hill*
- *Inspector Gadget*
- *The Librarian*

Books:

- *The Nerd Next Door* by Sylvie Stewart
- *The Perks of Being a Wallflower* by Stephen Chbosky
- *Were-Geeks Save Wisconsin* by Jade Lee
- *We Shouldn't* by Vi Keeland
- *Rock Bottom Girl* by Lucy Score
- *Queen of Klutz* by Samantha Garman

12

COLD/SERIOUS/UPTIGHT HERO/HEROINE

DEFINITION

In this trope, a character commences the story acting, and perhaps actually being, unemotional, detached, or tense in general. Over the course of the story, this character either loosens up enough to be able to fall in love, or the act of falling in love cracks the layer of ice around their heart, and the love itself loosens them up into a warmer, caring, more easygoing character. This is purely a trope of personal transformation, of overcoming personal issues that prevent the character from being able and willing to let themselves love.

NOTE: This trope also works as a character theme, where the character remains cold, serious, and uptight throughout the story, but still manages to find love without ever changing their personality. In this case, some other trope must do the work of creating obstacles to love that must be overcome.

ADJACENT TROPES

--Grumpy/Sunshine
--Redemption
--Oblivious to Love

--Lone Wolf Tamed

WHY READERS/VIEWERS LOVE THIS TROPE

--only for you does the cold, uptight character emerge from their protective emotional shell

--being let into the secret inner sanctum of this character's heart and mind

--I'm so special that he/she changed for me

--he/she is devoted solely and completely to me

OBLIGATORY SCENES
THE BEGINNING:

The coldness, seriousness, or uptightness of the main character is established. This is usually a character who hurts the people around him or her, or who, at a minimum, is off-putting to others. This behavior upsets, injures, or angers the potential love interest. True love between the cold, humorless, tense hero/heroine and their love interest seems impossible, and furthermore, the cold character isn't interested in love anyway.

THE MIDDLE:

Two things must happen in the middle of this story:

1. The cold/serious, uptight character must flirt with the idea of letting down his or her guard. They may experiment with small moments of relaxation or warmth, and they may push themselves to come out of their shell.
2. The love interest must attempt to break through the emotional walls this cold, serious, tense character has erected to protect themselves.

In the case of the clumsy, bumbling hero/heroine, that character is willing and eager to fall in love and is typically pursuing it aggressively, but with disastrous results. But in this case, the cold/serious hero/heroine is emotionally cut off from the notion of allowing themselves to love and refuses to participate willingly or eagerly in courting rituals, flirtation, and moments of physical attraction that would all typically lead to love blossoming. The potential love interest must do all the heavy lifting at trying to develop the relationship toward love for some or all of the middle of the story.

BLACK MOMENT:

Either the cold/serious/uptight hero/heroine refuses to let go of their emotional armor and succumb to love, or the love interest has had enough and gives up on ever getting through the emotional barriers the cold/serious/uptight hero/heroine has erected. In both cases, the relationship is an utter failure and all appears lost.

THE END:

Either the cold/serious/uptight hero/heroine finally gives in and allows love into their heart, or the love interest finally unlocks the key to getting through to the cold character and successfully convinces them to let go of their tight emotional control and fall in love.

The transformation of the cold/serious/uptight hero/heroine is complete, and true love and happily ever after are not only possible but achieved.

KEY SCENES

--the cold, uptight character's clear-headedness and cool logic save the day for the more emotional, hot-headed love interest

--the cold uptight character's first smile or first laugh

-- (in some stories) the cold, uptight character loses his or her temper

-- the cold, uptight hero runs very, very hot in a romantic or sexual situation

THINGS TO THINK ABOUT WHEN WRITING THIS TROPE

What is this character cold, serious, or uptight about? Is it everything in their lives, or some aspect in particular? Is it only love he or she is cold, serious, and uptight about? Or are there other things they treat similarly?

What makes this character likable to readers or viewers?

What makes this character worth the fight to their potential love interest? What compelling reason does the love interest have to stick around and fight through all the minefields this type of hero/heroine is going to erect between themselves and love?

What does this character have against love? What trauma in their past has turned them off to love? Has that trauma made them wary of other emotions as well? If so, which ones?

In what ways does this character's coldness, remoteness, and seriousness help them in life? How does this reinforce their desire not to change?

What are several secondary things that the cold/serious/uptight hero/heroine associates with love that they're also cold, serious, or uptight about? How can you work those into your story as well?

What are some physical objects or actions that reflect or symbolize the emotional fortress the cold/serious/uptight hero/heroine has built around himself or herself? How can you work those into the story?

Why is the love interest so persistent about breaking through to this closed off person? What in their personality and/or past drives them to keep going when they seem to be getting nowhere?

What is that one trigger that finally gets past the cold/serious/uptight hero/heroine's emotional defenses and forces them to acknowledge, feel, and allow love into their heart and mind? What is *that* trigger? Why is it so significant to this character?

How will the love interest pull that emotional trigger and how will it symbolize the breaking down of walls between these two characters?

What does the cold/serious/uptight hero/heroine's utter capitulation and surrender to love look like? Is it joyful? Wrenching? Cathartic? A release of pent-up grief or rage?

TROPE TRAPS

Creating so cold and unlikable a character that your reader hates them and stops reading your story.

Creating so wounded a character that only years of intensive therapy might even begin to plausibly breach the emotional walls this character has built around themselves.

Surrounding the cold/serious/uptight hero/heroine with characters that reinforce their emotional remoteness so strongly or trigger them so badly that the love interest can't plausibly get through to them.

Not creating a compelling enough reason for the love interest to stick it out and keep fighting to get through to the cold/serious/uptight hero/heroine. No matter how hot or rich a person might be, at some point it's just not worth the misery of continuing to bang one's head against that brick wall of solitude.

Not giving the reader a satisfying enough conclusion when the breakthrough finally happens for this character. Not only has their love interest been through the wringer, but so has the reader. They both deserve total surrender to love from this character.

Not creating a compelling and interesting means of finally reaching this character's heart and mind.

Creating too huge a personality reversal in the end to be believable. Human beings don't shift from utterly cold, serious, and uptight to warm, silly, and the life of the party overnight (or at all). This character is likely to retain some of his/her reserve or remoteness in some aspects of their life or regarding some people.

COLD/SERIOUS/UPTIGHT   HERO/HEROINE TROPE IN ACTION
Movies:

- *Risky Business*
- *Pretty Woman*
- *When Harry Met Sally*
- *Along Came Polly*

Books:

- *The Favor* by Suzanne Wright
- *Her Best Worst Mistake* by Sarah Mayberry
- *Mr. Masters* by T. L. Swan
- *To Have and To Hate* by R. S. Grey
- *Make Me Sin* by J.T. Geissinger
- *Conspiracy* by Lindsay Buroker

13

COMMITMENT PHOBIA

DEFINITION

The hero or heroine in this trope cannot commit to a permanent relationship. They may be fine with flirtation, romance, and even falling in love. But for some compelling reason, this character cannot pull the trigger and say, "I do,"... or at least commit to a forever after.

Although this trope is included in a book on internal tropes, it's entirely possible that the cause of this commitment phobia is external to the phobic character, meaning some outside event, person, force, or situation has caused this character's internal fear of commitment.

This is a trope of personal transformation as the commitment-phobe overcomes their fears and learns to commit to love and to a long-term relationship.

ADJACENT TROPES

--Right Under Your Nose
--On the Run
--Oblivious to Love
--Reclusive Hero/Heroine

. . .

WHY READERS/VIEWERS LOVE THIS TROPE

--overcoming your fears to find true love

--he or she will change for you

--you healed the person no one else could

--you landed the big fish or trophy that no one else could

OBLIGATORY SCENES
THE BEGINNING:

This story type may begin with the commitment phobic hero or heroine launching into a relationship with no sign of their phobia ... yet. They may even be enthusiastic about the process of falling in love.

This story may also begin with the commitment phobic hero or heroine exhibiting fear of this relationship, or all relationships, immediately.

Lastly, this story may begin with the commitment phobic hero or heroine entering into a relationship with some degree of caution. And, at the first sign that this has the potential to become a permanent relationship, they balk.

THE MIDDLE:

The relationship develops well. Very well. Far too well, in fact, for the commitment phobic character. The developing romance goes to war with the hero/heroine's fear of commitment.

The love interest begins to see the cracks in the commitment-phobe character and to realize that the person they're falling for may be a serious flight risk.

BLACK MOMENT:

The moment of commitment has arrived. This may come in the form of a proposal, or at the altar in the form of an "I do," or simply a promise of forever to their partner. But in each case, the commitment phobic character panics and fails to commit.

All is lost. The relationship appears over. The partner who has just been abandoned is done waiting around for the commitment-phobe to get his or her act together.

THE END:

The thought of losing their partner is too much for the commit-ment-phobe to bear. They find a way to overcome their fear or they have some kind of emotional breakthrough that allows them, finally, to commit to their partner, and to be happy about doing so.

KEY SCENES

--the first moment of panic for the commitment-phobe

--the first inkling by the love interest that all is not as it seems on the surface with their romantic partner.

--moment of regret by the commitment-phobe

--moment of forgiveness by the love interest of the commitment-phobe

--the moment of fleeing the scene (and the love interest) by the commitment-phobe

THINGS TO THINK ABOUT WHEN WRITING THIS TROPE

Why is the commitment phobic character afraid to commit to a long-term relationship? Is there some trauma in his or her own past to make them fear love? Has he or she witnessed something with family or friends to make them fear commitment? Has this character been burned by love before? Who burned them? Why?

Is the cause of the hero/heroine's commitment phobia external in origin, meaning it's caused by circumstances, events, forces, or people around them? For example, he or she must marry for some reason and resents or rejects that reason. Or is it internal in origin, meaning it stems from fears or trauma within the commitment-phobe's psyche?

What is the outward manifestation of this commitment phobia? Is the character distant in his or her relationships? Cold? Cruel? Shut down? Flirtatious? Fickle? Wild? Unpredictable?

When does the romantic partner of the commitment-phobe realize there's a problem? Does he or she know from the very beginning? Or are they into the relationship a bit before they glimpse storm clouds on the horizon? Or are they stunned at the moment of commitment?

How does the romantic partner of the commitment-phobe react when their partner balks at following through on the relationship? How do others around the couple react to it?

Is there a compelling reason above and beyond true love for their romantic partner to prompt the commitment-phobe to finally conquer their fear?

How will the commitment-phobe overcome their fear? Is there some external problem they have to fix? Is there some internal demon they finally have to face and conquer? What does that battle look like? How ugly does it get?

How and why will the partner of the commitment-phobe forgive them for balking at commitment in the first place? What will that forgiveness look like?

Why should the romantic partner of the commitment-phobe trust them when they finally commit? How will the phobic character convince their love interest of their sincerity and total commitment? What grand gesture will they make to show their true and abiding love?

TROPE TRAPS

Not creating a compelling enough reason for the commitment-phobe to actually be phobic of commitment.

The commitment-phobe coming across as arrogant or selfish instead of truly afraid of commitment.

Creating a character who's deeply unlikable because of their unwillingness to commit to a totally lovable partner. And, secondarily, the audience cheering against the commitment-phobe and wanting the romantic partner to run, not walk, away from the commitment-phobe.

Failing to create a believable means for the commitment-phobe to overcome their fear. A big fear requires a big effort to overcome it.

The romantic partner looking weak for taking back (too easily) the character who has rejected them and rejected commitment to them.

Creating romantic-partner characters with low enough self-esteem to make them unlikable to readers or viewers.

The reader feeling whiplashed when a romance appears to be progressing just fine and then, abruptly and without warning, the commitment-phobe reveals himself or herself. It's fine to surprise your audience along with surprising the romantic interest, but the reasons for the commitment-phobe feeling the way they do have to be extra-plausible in this scenario.

Most of us know one or more commitment-phobes, and we know they rarely change. The trap then, is failing to create a story that puts the hero/heroine through enough suffering to achieve real growth.

Confusing just wanting to fool around and have a good time with true fear of commitment. Play-now/commit later is not actually a fear of commitment. Also, the playboy/playgirl who'll get around to a real relationship later is often not likable to readers or viewers.

COMMITMENT PHOBIA TROPE IN ACTION
Movies:

- *Notting Hill*
- *Valentine's Day*

- *Alfie*
- *Sleeping with Other People*
- *Love, Guaranteed*

Books:

- *Wicked Intentions* by Elizabeth Hoyt
- *Until You* by Judith McNaught
- *The Naked Fisherman* by Jewel. E. Ann
- *Hate Me* by Ashley Jade
- *Married by Morning* by Lisa Kleypas
- *The Marriage Trap* by Jennifer Probst
- *On Dublin Street* by Samantha Young
- *Beautiful Stranger* by Christina Lauren
- *Ten Tiny Breaths* by K.A. Tucker
- *The Edge of Never* by J.A. Redmerski

14

DAMAGED/TRAUMATIZED/WOUNDED HERO/HEROINE

DEFINITION

This is a broad trope covering all kinds of emotional trauma, psychological damage, and/or physical damage. It's differentiated from the disabled hero/heroine because the damaged character can ultimately be healed fully, or at least to some degree, while the disabled hero/heroine's condition is permanent.

In this trope, the hero or heroine is damaged in some way. They may start the story damaged, or they may become damaged in the early part of the story. The arc of this character is always toward healing and/or coming to terms with their damage and making peace with it ... of course with the love, support, and help of their romantic partner.

ADJACENT TROPES
--Nursing Back to Health
--Disabled Hero/Heroine
--Recovery/Rehabilitation

. . .

WHY READERS/VIEWERS LOVE THIS TROPE
--having the power to heal a wounded soul

--giving oneself hope of one day being whole

--making the broken whole

--being accepted as one is without the pressure of needing to be perfect

--finding peace

--desire for self-acceptance and self-love

OBLIGATORY SCENES
THE BEGINNING:

This story can begin with the hero or heroine already damaged. The results of that damage may or may not be visible to others. It's also possible that this story starts with the moment of the damage being inflicted.

The romantic partner of the damaged character meets the damaged potential love interest and may or may not see the damage or its effect(s).

For some reason, the damaged character and potential romantic partner enter into a relationship.

THE MIDDLE:

The damage makes itself clearly known in the middle of the story. If everything was going well at first, this is where the damage starts to cause havoc.

The true toll of the damage is revealed, and the damaged character enters a downward spiral of being buried by the effects of the damage.

The romantic partner makes a valiant effort to hold their partner and the relationship together, but gradually, it all slips through this lovelorn soul's fingers.

There may be efforts to heal the damage in this stage of the story.

Depending on the type and severity of the damage your hero or heroine has suffered, they may or may not make progress toward healing in the middle of the story.

BLACK MOMENT:

Any treatment that has been underway fails utterly at this point. The hoped-for cure doesn't materialize, is a fraud, or for some reason doesn't work.

The damaged character falls completely apart, physically, emotionally, and/or psychologically. This may be the moment when the damage is dramatically (and humiliatingly) revealed to the world.

It's unlikely that the romantic partner is unaware of the damage before now, but it's technically possible that the reason for all the self-destructive and devastating behavior that has ruined the relationship may finally be fully explained now.

The damaged character flees or breaks off the relationship, and there appears to be no way back to any sort of happily ever after.

The romantic partner has done his or her best to help their partner, but all their efforts have failed.

THE END:

The damaged hero or heroine finally comes to grips with their damage, partially or completely healing it at last, or at least making peace with it in such a way that he or she can finally move forward with their life. Furthermore, he or she is now capable of participating in a healthy relationship and sustaining it for the long term.

The romantic partner forgives the damaged character and all is well. A hard-earned happily ever after is finally possible ... and achieved.

KEY SCENES

--hero/heroine discovers he/she is damaged and the extent of the damage

--damaged hero/heroine does something unforgivable to the love interest

--confession of unworthiness (to be loved) by damaged character

--moment of apology by damaged character

--moment of forgiveness by love interest that doesn't include getting back together

--acceptance of worthiness (to be loved) by damaged character

THINGS TO THINK ABOUT WHEN WRITING THIS TROPE

What kind of damage is your hero or heroine suffering from?

When did the damage occur? Before or after your story begins? How did it occur?

How will the emotional damage suffered by your character manifest itself in physical symptoms, behaviors, or tics? Will they overcome this behavior over the course of the story? For example, will this character always flinch at the sound of a loud explosion or get over it?

It's worth noting that, in his seminal book on trauma, *The Body Keeps the Score*, Dr. Bessel van der Kolk makes the argument that trauma rewires the brain permanently, changing forever how the body reacts to subsequent trauma or triggers from the original trauma.

You can absolutely write a hero or heroine who fully heals from their trauma and its aftermath, just be aware that modern science does not suggest that the brain can be un-wired from its responses to trauma. People learn to live with the rewired brain, to have proportional responses to triggers, and to live full and productive lives around and in spite of their trauma responses.

If your preference is to fully heal all emotional trauma to a hero or heroine, you are fictionalizing an ideal ending—which is perfectly fine to do. Just be aware that you will have readers and viewers who've experienced the trauma you're describing, and they may not achieve the same outcome. This will require special sensitivity on your part in handling your idealized outcome.

SIDE NOTE: exposing a traumatized person to similar situations to the one that caused the original trauma do not help in the healing process. Studies show that doing this only further traumatizes the victim. Be very careful of triggering readers or viewers if you take this approach in your story.

How aware of the damage is your damaged character to begin with? How aware of the damage is the romantic partner?

How does the damage affect your damaged character's life? How does the damage affect their romantic partner's life?

How do others react to the damaged character's damage?

What compellingly likable and lovable qualities does your damaged character have that make them worth the effort to stay with until they're more healed?

How little or how much do you plan to fudge the medical knowledge available to heal your character's damage in the time period the story takes place in? For the sake of your story, you may choose to take medical liberties so your damaged character can fully heal by the end of the story.

What form will this treatment and healing process take? Will the love interest administer the treatment, or will an outside medical professional get involved?

How will the love interest interact with the hero/heroine's damage? With sympathy? Empathy? Pity? Fear?

What qualities does the love interest see in the damaged hero/heroine that makes them worth the effort, pain, and risk of loving and trying to heal?

TROPE TRAPS

Creating a damaged hero or heroine who is so dark and so devoid of redeeming qualities that they become unlikable and not plausibly lovable.

Letting the lashing out in pain of a damaged hero or heroine cross over into the realm of emotional or physical abuse of their romantic interest.

Letting a romantic partner stick around and take abuse long after they reasonably should have left the situation. Real care must be taken by the author in regard to this one. **Ethically, you owe it to your reader not to advocate that they stay in an abusive relationship, nor to advocate staying because someday it might miraculously get better**.

Creating an unbelievable trauma and unrealistic trauma response. Yes, this is fiction, but with regard to some topics, fiction must be more believable than real life for readers or viewers to buy into your premise.

Unrealistically fast or miraculous healing of the damage or trauma.

Creating a love interest who is not sufficiently sympathetic to the damaged hero or heroine's struggle. Or conversely, creating a love interest who miraculously knows exactly what to do to heal the damaged hero or heroine, in spite of having no medical or psychological knowledge at all.

DAMAGED/TRAUMATIZED/WOUNDED HERO/HEROINE TROPE IN ACTION
Movies:

- *Dr. Strange*
- *The English Patient*
- *A Star is Born*
- *Manchester by the Sea*

Books:

- *Flowers from the Storm* by Laura Kinsale
- *Archer's Voice* by Mia Sheridan
- *Lover Awakened* by J.R. Ward
- *Vicious* by L.J. Shen
- *Bared to You* by Sylvia Day
- *Credence* by Penelope Douglas
- *Ugly Love* by Colleen Hoover
- *The Deal* by Elle Kennedy
- *One Dublin Street* by Samantha Young
- *Cry Wolf* by Patricia Briggs

15

DANGEROUS SECRET

DEFINITION

In this trope, the hero or heroine is keeping a secret that is eventually revealed. The keeping of the secret or the revealing of the secret —or both—cause havoc with the love story. This negative reaction to the revealed secret must be overcome for the hero and heroine to eventually find their happily ever after.

Some dangerous secrets are so archetypal that they have broken out into their own tropes: secret babies, secret relationships, secret identities, secret worlds, secret pregnancies, secret marriages, and secret crushes to name a few.

For an essentially honest and honorable person, keeping a dangerous secret may be very difficult, or very easy, depending on the nature of the secret. But the existence of a secret is as much a moral crisis as a crisis of damaging or painful information becoming known.

There are a bunch of variations on what kind of secret this might be, who's keeping it, who else knows about it, who it'll affect, and what kind of damage it will do when made public, and we'll explore those in a minute.

The one thing to realize, though, is the dangerous secret is ALWAYS revealed. If a character has a secret and successfully keeps it, then it's likely to have little or no effect on the love story between that character and their love interest. Therefore, it's not a romance trope.

One might argue that the person keeping the secret could be tortured by guilt or the burden of keeping the secret which could greatly affect a relationship, and you would not be wrong. But a guilty character or a tortured character is a character type, not a full-blown trope with a beginning, middle, and end.

For a dangerous secret to be trope and have the movement necessary to carry a story arc, that secret must ultimately come out.

Worth thinking about: Secrets have a tendency to become more dangerous and more difficult to reveal the longer a person keeps them. The potential consequences have a way of growing and growing inside the mind of the person keeping the secret. Which is to say, time is the enemy of easily, honestly, and forthrightly revealing a secret. The longer it festers, the more internal damage it typically does to the secret keeper, and the more external damage it potentially does when revealed.

At its core, this is a trope of moral crisis and resolution of that crisis so that unburdened true love is possible.

ADJACENT TROPES
--Secret Baby
--Secret Crush
--Secret Marriage
--Secret Identity
--Secret World
--Disguised as a Male/Female

WHY READERS/VIEWERS LOVE THIS TROPE
-- who doesn't love a good scandal, bit of gossip, or juicy bit of news

-- being in on the big secret that nobody else knows

--eagerly anticipating how everyone will react when it's finally revealed

--enjoyment of a big fight that I'm not in the middle of but can sit back and watch the show

--he/she confesses just for you

--receiving unconditional trust (given to the love interest by the person revealing the secret to them)

OBLIGATORY SCENES
THE BEGINNING:

The hero and heroine meet and attraction sparks between them. This could be The One. The hero and heroine definitely are interested in spending more time together. Small problem: one of them has a secret reason for this potential relationship being a big problem.

While the secret itself is often not revealed in the beginning, the fact that there is a secret is almost without exception established fairly quickly. The scale of the secret, who it would affect if it leaks, and the extent of damage it could cause are typically revealed. However, this information may be unreliable if it comes from the hero or heroine keeping the secret. The imagined damage may be far greater than the actual damage when the secret finally comes out.

The love interest is established as not knowing the secret.

Everyone else who knows and doesn't know about the secret may be established.

The reader may or may not be let in on exactly what the secret is.

THE MIDDLE:

If the details about the secret haven't been established for the reader yet, they are now. The stakes of revealing the secret and not revealing the secret are established. How big a secret is it? Who knows it? Who doesn't know it? How bad will it be if the secret becomes public?

The difficulty of keeping the secret becomes clear, and the hero or heroine burdened with keeping this secret may be starting to suffer the ill effects of carrying it around. As the romance develops, an ever-increasing need to tell the secret resides in the hero or heroine. And it secretly drives them crazy. They are torn between protecting the secret and telling all to the person they're falling for.

The love interest may suspect there's a secret lurking somewhere. The love interest may sense or somehow know that the hero/heroine isn't telling the whole truth or may be withholding something big. This causes increasing tension between the lovers. Meanwhile, the secret swirls through everyone's lives, demanding release more and more stridently.

The hero or heroine keeping the secret approaches a moral crisis of having to choose between the person they're falling in love with and keeping the secret. The need to reveal the dangerous secret becomes nearly unbearable.

BLACK MOMENT:

The secret comes out. Any number of people may reveal the secret in any number of ways. The consequences of the secret explode across your story, and its revelation tears the lovers apart.

Perhaps the secret itself has the power to destroy the relationship. Or perhaps the act of keeping the secret destroys the trust between the lovers. Maybe outsiders affected by the secret tear the lovers apart. But in any case, the relationship appears completely ruined and finished in the wake of the secret's unveiling.

THE END:

The fallout from the secret coming out is finally contained and dealt with. Any damage done by the secret being revealed is fixed, or the lovers have at least put the damage behind them.

The former secret keeper is relieved to be free of the burden of the secret. He or she makes amends and apologies for lying or withholding the truth. The love interest finds it in his or her heart to forgive the secret keeper, and the lovers are finally reunited. With the air clean between them, they can now move forward into the future with trust and have their happily ever after.

KEY SCENES

--the reader finding out what the big secret is

--the love interest finding out there is a secret being kept from him or her

--the love interest finding out what the big secret is

--the big apology for having kept a secret

THINGS TO THINK ABOUT WHEN WRITING THIS TROPE

Obviously, the first question must address what the dangerous secret the hero or heroine is keeping is. How dangerous is it, really?

Does it regard past, present, or future events and people? If in the past, how far in the past? If in the future, how far in the future will this secret come into play? Who has already been affected by this secret? Who will be affected by it in the future?

How dangerous does the hero or heroine believe the secret is? Are they right? If not, why not?

Who else besides the hero or heroine knows about the secret? How did they find out about it?

Is it a personal secret, or are its stakes larger than that? Is it a national secret? Classified information? A business secret? A skeleton in the family closet? Something that only the hero or heroine knows and has never told another living soul?

What will, in fact, happen when the dangerous secret is revealed? What does the hero or heroine (possibly wrongly) believe or fear will happen when the secret is revealed?

Who else will be affected, and how, by the revelation of the dangerous secret? Is the hero or heroine keeping the secret willingly to harm those people in that way? Why? If not, why not?

Is this dangerous secret the hero's or heroine's to keep? Does he or she need permission from someone else to reveal the secret? If so, who?

How do the other people who know about the secret feel about it being revealed by the hero or heroine?

Once the love interest is let in on the secret, will he or she become part of the conspiracy of silence to go on protecting the secret? Or will the secret become public at that point?

Does anyone in on it joke obliquely about the secret or make veiled references to it in front of others and make the secret keeper massively uncomfortable?

When in your story will you reveal the secret to your reader or viewer? How will you do the big reveal? Is this a big, climactic moment in the story or not?

To whom in the story is the dangerous secret first revealed? By whom is it first revealed? Does the hero or heroine keeping the dangerous secret get there first, or does someone else reveal the dangerous secret to the love interest? If so, what does the love interest think about that?

How does the person revealing the secret reveal it? Is there a serious conversation prefaced by a warning of a big thing to discuss? Does it come out in the heat of an argument or the heat of sex? Does it slip out by accident?

How does the love interest react to the secret?

How does the love interest react to the fact that the hero/heroine didn't tell them the secret initially, but has revealed it to them now?

Does the secret-keeping hero or heroine owe the love interest an apology? If so, how big an apology? How will he or she deliver it? Is the apology big enough to make up for the size of the deception?

Does the secret keeper lie outright to protect the secret? Does he or she evade the subject, dodge hard questions, or speak in half-truths? Does he or she believe they're lying by withholding the truth?

What kind of moral compass does the secret keeper have, and how does keeping this secret affect him or her?

TROPE TRAPS

Not creating a dangerous enough secret to justify keeping the secret for most of your story.

The dangerous secret isn't actually dangerous. The world wouldn't end, and the relationship wouldn't be doomed if the secret is revealed.

Two mature adults could reasonably sit down and talk out the secret, coming to an understanding about it and why it was kept secret that wouldn't wreck the relationship.

Making so many people aware of the secret that it's incredibly implausible someone didn't blab it long ago. After all, humans are notoriously bad at keeping secrets, and most people can't actually keep a big secret for any length of time.

The secret keeper ultimately revealing a secret that's not rightfully theirs to keep or tell. That's not the least bit heroic and will require quite a redemption arc. Breach of trust is very difficult for any relationship to survive.

Revealing the secret in a lame way that's not worthy of the hero/heroine's buildup of its importance in their own mind.

Failing to resolve the external crisis created by the secret being made known to others.

Failing to show the full fallout of the secret becoming public (or the full fallout of the hero/heroine and love interest going forward together while keeping the secret together.)

· · ·

DANGEROUS SECRET TROPE IN ACTION
Movies:

- *True Lies*
- *Man of Steel*
- *Bohemian Rhapsody*
- *Can You Keep A Secret?*
- *Jane Eyre*
- *Notes On A Scandal*
- *Sister of the Groom*

Books:

- *Only Ever Her* by Marybeth Mayhew Whalen
- *Little Fires Everywhere* by Celeste Ng
- *The Joy Luck Club* by Amy Tan
- *The Secret Place* by Tana French
- *Big Little Lies* by Liane Moriarty
- *A Discovery of Witches* by Deborah Harkness
- *The Keeper of Lost Things* by Ruth Hogan
- *The Book of Lost Things* by John Connolly
- *Her Fearful Symmetry* by Audrey Niffenegger
- *The Vanishing Act of Esme Lennox* by Maggie O'Farrell
- *The House at Riverton* by Kate Morton

16
DISABLED HERO/HEROINE

DEFINITION

Unlike the damaged/traumatized hero or heroine, the disabled hero or heroine has a permanent disability that cannot be healed. The emphasis of this trope is learning to live with, making peace with, or achieving one's goals with a disability. Whereas the damaged/traumatized hero/heroine trope is, at its core about healing, this trope is, at its core about living to the fullest.

In this trope, the hero or heroine has a challenge of some kind to overcome in life. At its core, this is a trope of steadfastness, of courage, of staying the course. The love interest's job is to support this journey or come to support it, and to love the hero/heroine not only in spite of their disability, but because of it and because of how they deal with it.

ADJACENT TROPES
  --Nursing Back to Health
  --Damaged Hero/Heroine
  --Recovery/Rehabilitation

. . .

WHY READERS/VIEWERS LOVE THIS TROPE

--being loved as you are

--overcoming adversity and achieving triumph

--feeling better about your life in comparison to the struggles of someone else's life

--everyone is lovable

OBLIGATORY SCENES

THE BEGINNING:

Clearly, the hero or heroine either begins the story with a disability or acquires one in the beginning portion of the story. Limitations of the disability are established. These may be overcome later, but they are not overcome in the beginning.

The love interest may be an existing love interest before the disability becomes part of the relationship, or the love interest may meet the hero/heroine after a disability is acquired.

In some stories, the disabled hero/heroine sets a goal for himself or herself that is very difficult or appears impossible at first. NOTE: This doesn't have to be something as lofty as becoming an Olympic athlete. It can be as simple as doing something independently for oneself or finding one's own happily ever after.

THE MIDDLE:

The challenges of the disability become evident and must be faced. There are likely to be successes and/or failures along the way. If the main arc of the story is dealing with the disability, the middle is where those issues come up. If the disability is secondary to the main storyline, the disability is likely to get in the way of the hero/heroine accomplishing the goal(s) of the main plot.

The love interest grapples with their role in dealing with the hero/heroine's disability. The love interest may not get it right initially.

The love story between the main characters begins to develop, but the disability may turn into a third wheel in their relationship.

BLACK MOMENT:

The disabled hero/heroine fails at their goal.

The disability proves to be an insurmountable obstacle in the plot and/or in the hero and heroine's relationship.

The lovers are defeated and cannot find a way to their happily ever after.

THE END:

The tides turn, victory is achieved. The disability itself is overcome (as in mastery over it is achieved, accommodation to it is achieved, or making peace with it and with self is achieved). The goal the hero/heroine has set for himself/herself is achieved. Perhaps the disabled character works around their disability to achieve their goal, or perhaps the disability itself turns into a hidden strength and helps him/her achieve their goal.

The lovers find their way back together in spite of the disability, because of the disability, or completely without the disability being a factor any longer.

KEY SCENES

--moment of individual despair by each main character

--moment of rage by the disabled character and possibly the love interest

--moment of acceptance of the unchangeable situation by each character

--moment of humor regarding the disability between the main characters

. . .

THINGS TO THINK ABOUT WHEN WRITING THIS TROPE

What kind of disability does the hero or heroine have? How does it impact their life?

How does this character become disabled?

When does the hero/heroine become disabled? Has he/she lived with it for a long time, has it happened recently before your story begins, or does it happen during your story?

What limitations does this disability place on the hero/heroine? What secondary, less obvious limitations are a side effect of that main disability? What perceived limitations does the hero/heroine believe they have that, in fact, they do not have or they can overcome?

Are there hidden benefits that arise from this disability?

How does the disabled character feel about their disability?

Does the disabled hero/heroine have a goal they're aiming toward that the disability impacts their ability to achieve?

How does the love interest feel about the disability and/or people with this disability?

How much or how little will the love interest be involved with the hero/heroine's big goal(s)?

What lessons does the love interest learn by observing how the hero/heroine goes about life?

How much of a factor will the disability be in the love story between these two people?

How does the disability interfere with or enable the love story?

Does this story have realistic ups AND downs of life with this particular disability?

TROPE TRAPS

Beware of giving the love interest a savior complex. Real love is based on respect, not pity.

Writing a so persistently uplifting or depressing tale that people who actually have this disability come after you for failure to do research or learn about the disability and its effects.

Failing to ever give the disabled hero/heroine moments of doubt, sadness, resentment, etc. Conversely, failing to give the hero/heroine moments of humor, courage, strength, joy, etc.

Rushing the accomplishment of genuinely challenging goals

Writing the hero/heroine as a personification of a disability and not a fully formed person who happens to have a disability.

DISABLED HERO/HEROINE TROPE IN ACTION MOVIES:

- *Me Before You*
- *The Theory of Everything*
- *The Way He Looks*
- *Still Alice*
- *Inside I'm Dancing*
- *I Am Sam*
- *My Left Foot*

BOOKS:

- *Devil in Winter* by Lisa Kleypas
- *Me Before You* by Jojo Moyes
- *Lover Enshrined* by J.R. Ward
- *Mine* by Katy Evans
- *The Unsung Hero* by Suzanne Brockmann
- *Rules of Attraction* by Simone Elkeles
- *Maybe Someday* by Colleen Hoover
- *Archer's Voice* by Mia Sheridan
- *The Duke and I* by Julia Quinn

17

FEAR OF INTIMACY

DEFINITION

This trope is driven by the hero and/or the heroine's fears. One or both of them is afraid to draw close to another person in a romantic relationship, and their journey(s) from fear to ability to engage in an intimate relationship shapes the arc of this trope. The core of this arc is personal transformation.

This trope often starts from a place of trauma. After all, desire to love and be loved is one of the deepest and most fundamental human desires.

ADJACENT TROPES

--Shy Hero/Heroine
--Virgin Hero/Heroine
--Burned by Love
--Celibate Hero/Heroine
--Reclusive Hero/Heroine

WHY READERS/VIEWERS LOVE THIS TROPE

--healing a wounded soul

--changed/fixed themselves for you

--being given a special gift no one else can have

--creation of a secret world

OBLIGATORY SCENES
THE BEGINNING:

This type of hero or heroine begins the story avoiding that which they fear. They live in a steady or even frozen state that does not include the intimacy that so terrifies them. This intimacy-free world is established to give the reader a frame of reference from which to see the character's growth later on.

Somebody or something challenges the fearful character to do something that will bring up a risk of intimacy. For example, a parent tells a young woman she must marry, like it or not. A hero realizes he must have a wife to succeed in his career but is terrified of relationships.

A compelling reason for the hero or heroine to *have* to overcome their fear of intimacy is established.

THE MIDDLE:

The reluctant hero or heroine is thrown into a situation whose likely outcome is intimacy ... whereupon their fear explodes. The middle of this type of story will be a continuous dance of advance and retreat. The fearful character will move toward the object of potential intimacy and then jerk away, unable to overcome their fear. They'll repeat this cycle over and over.

At some point during this dance, the reason why the hero or heroine is afraid of intimacy will be revealed. This revelation is often a major turning point in the story, as now the other partner knows exactly what they're up against and can actively engage in helping the fearful partner, who can now consciously attempt to overcome their fear.

BLACK MOMENT:

The character afraid of intimacy has almost managed to overcome their fear, but at the critical moment, pulls away one last time. It appears all is lost and that this person will never truly be able to overcome their fear to find the happiness that lies beyond it.

THE END:

Ultimately, the fearful person's love for their partner gives them the strength to overcome their fear once and for all. It may be that the source of the fear is finally faced and dealt with, or simply that the fearful hero or heroine finally finds the strength to overpower their fear.

KEY SCENES

--the source of the fear is triggered

--a panic attack by the fearful character

--the source of the fear is revealed

--confession of fear by fearful character

--love interest's first success at breaking through the main character's wall of fear.

THINGS TO THINK ABOUT WHEN WRITING THIS TROPE

What truly compelling reason does the fearful hero or heroine have to finally confront their fear of intimacy? Overcoming a fear of this kind is a monumental challenge, and it's going to take a really strong motivation to push the fearful hero or heroine forward into facing their fear.

Is the fearful person's fear of intimacy rational or irrational?

What is the cause of their fear of intimacy? When in your story does it make sense to reveal what the core cause of this fear is?

How will the other partner in the relationship feel about and react to the hero or heroine's fear of intimacy?

What sort of problems will the hero or heroine's fear of intimacy introduce into the relationship?

What tactics will the other partner employ to overcome the hero or heroine's fear?

What will failure to overcome their fear look like to the hero or heroine? (This may define your black moment.)

What are the stakes if the fearful hero or heroine fails to overcome their fear?

What is the would-be romantic partner's motivation to hang in there until the fearful hero or heroine sorts out their issues?

The would-be romantic partner of a hero or heroine afraid of intimacy is going to have to be exceptionally patient and exceptionally motivated to stick out the ups and downs of a relationship with this kind of character. What will that look like in your story? How frustrated will the love interest be over the course of the story?

What strongly positive effects of succeeding to break through the partner's fear of intimacy will motivate the love interest? Likewise, what negative effects of failing to reach past the hero/heroine's fear motivates the love interest?

Why is the love interest irresistibly drawn to a person this difficult to draw into love? What is it about the love interest that makes them interested in and willing to take on the challenge of a lover afraid of intimacy?

What's in this relationship for the love interest? What will they get out of it—either emotionally, materially, or psychologically?

Is the fearful hero/heroine aware of how much they're withholding from their partner? How do they feel about that? What do they ultimately do about it?

Does the fearful hero/heroine's newfound ability to connect intimately extend beyond the love interest, or is it only for that one person in their life?

TROPE TRAPS

Failing to create strong enough motivation for the fearful character to change. It's not enough for a fearful character to be interested in self-improvement. If that's all the motivation it takes for your hero or heroine to face their fear of intimacy, then the cause of their fear isn't nearly strong enough to sustain an entire arc in a story.

Creating too weak a back story in the development of this wounded soul. It takes real trauma to put people completely off of wanting intimacy and love.

Introducing the fearful character's backstory at the wrong time and failing to maximize the impact of that revelation.

Drawing too impatient a love interest for fearful hero/heroine.

Creating a hero/heroine who's so unwilling to change that they're unbelievable or so pathetic they aren't heroic.

Most of us know people with a deep fear of intimacy, and they rarely change. Failing to convince the reader that the fearful hero/heroine has gone through enough to truly change.

Failing to create devastating enough consequences if the love interest fails to break through the hero/heroine's fear of intimacy.

Not painting the full emotional cost to the love interest of the fearful partner's inability to connect intimately.

FEAR OF INTIMACY TROPE IN ACTION
Movies:

- *The 40-Year-Old Virgin*

- *Eat Pray Love*
- *The Conversation*
- *Wild Orchid*
- *On Chesil Beach*
- *The Chambermaid Lynn*

Books:

- *Twilight* by Stephanie Meyers
- *Lord Satyr* by Jade Lee
- *Then Came You* by Lisa Kleypas
- *Run from Fear* by Jami Alden
- *False Start* by Marianne Rice

18

FRESH START/DO-OVER

DEFINITION

In this story, the hero or the heroine is completely resetting and restarting his or her life. This may be a voluntary decision or it may have been forced upon him or her. It's a clean slate, a full do-over of a life. In the midst of this radical personal transformation, a love interest shows up, either to complicate matters or to enrich the hero/heroine's new life and make it complete.

The person making a fresh start may stay geographically in the same location and live among the same people. However, he or she may start a new job, take a radically new approach to old relationships, or choose to deal with his or her life in a whole new way.

The love interest can be a leftover of the hero or heroine's old life. Or the love interest may be a new relationship that's part of the new life the hero/heroine is making for himself or herself.

This story can follow several different arcs. In one, the hero/heroine's old life may show up at some point (in the form of a person, problem, or threat) to mess up the fresh start. In spite of the hero/heroine's resolve to start over, he or she is now forced to deal with old, unresolved problems he or she hoped to have walked away from.

In another version of this story, the hero/heroine experiences enough personal growth or has enough time to solve the previously unsolvable problem(s) of his or her old life. After having taken this break, he or she decides to return to the old life, deal with the problem(s), and convince the new love interest to stay with him or her in the old life.

In yet another version of this trope, the hero/heroine has left behind an old life in its entirety and resolutely moves forward in his or her new life. IN this case, it's more likely that the hoer/heroine has physically left behind the old life and is making a fresh new start in a whole new place. He or she may eventually reveal to the new love interest what the past was like and may need to deal with leftover trauma and scars from his or her past, but the hero/heroine never returns to the old life. This main character may struggle to move forward into the fresh start and leave behind the past, and this effort becomes the main focus of the story's conflict.

At its core, this is a trope or personal transformation, of redefining self, of choosing to leave behind the past entirely and strike out in a new personal direction. It typically includes making peace with the past and putting it to rest so the lovers can move forward into a new and brighter future and happily ever after.

ADJACENT TROPES
--Running Away from Home
--Amnesia
--Makeover
--On the Run
--Following Your Heart

WHY READERS/VIEWERS LOVE THIS TROPE
--walking away from all your problems and leaving them behind
--totally reinventing who you are and how others perceive you

--falling for a mysterious stranger

--being let into someone's secret world and secret past

--the rolling stone loves you enough to settle down and stay in one place for you

OBLIGATORY SCENES
THE BEGINNING:

This story may begin at the point of the hero/heroine walking away from his or her old life. We may get a glimpse of his or her old life and the reason(s) why he or she is choosing to or being forced to walk away.

This story may begin after the hero/heroine has walked away—physically or metaphorically—from his or her past life. In this case, you probably won't show the audience anything about this person's past right away. Rather, you'll let the audience discover this person's secrets, scars, trauma, and history along with the new love interest.

In either case, the hero/heroine meets the love interest. If this is a new person in the hero/heroine's life, they can meet pretty much any way you can imagine. The tone of this meeting (humorous, light-hearted, tense, dangerous) will set the tone for the rest of your story.

If the love interest is part of the hero/heroine's past, the love interest shows up in the hero/heroine's new life, typically as a surprise. This may or may not be a pleasant surprise for the hero/heroine—a choice which will set much of the tone of your story.

THE MIDDLE:

The hero/heroine and love interest commence spending time together and falling in love. The external plot of your story usually sets these characters up to spend time together on an ongoing basis so they have a chance to get to know each other.

The love interest figures out the hero/heroine has walked away from his or her past and is starting a new life. The love interest naturally wants to know everything about this person he or she is falling for hard and will attempt to learn more about the hero/heroine's past. The hero/heroine may try to block this research (or snooping, as the case may be) and may not cooperate with any of it.

Friends and family of the love interest may object to him or her falling for this stranger whom they know so little about.

Internal conflict builds between the hero/heroine and love interest. The love interest may resent the hero/heroine's refusal to share much or any information about his or her past. The hero/heroine may wrestle with demons out of his or her past and push away the new love interest because of them.

The past pursues the hero/heroine whether he or she likes it or not. Old trauma, threats, scars, problems, or people may surface to cause trouble. They may cause trouble only for the hero/heroine, or they may also cause serious trouble for the love interest, up to and including putting the love interest's life in serious danger.

As the past and its troubles build toward a crisis, the hero/heroine must seriously consider leaving again and trying to make yet another fresh start somewhere else or in some other way, if for no other reason than to protect the love interest with whom they've fallen in love. The love interest may sense this impulse to leave and be deeply stressed out about the hero/heroine as a flight risk.

BLACK MOMENT:

The past catches up with the hero/heroine in spite of his or her best efforts to leave it behind and make a fresh start. The love interest may be endangered or harmed. The hero/heroine's attempt to walk away from the past has failed. He or she can't escape whatever he or she was trying to get away from.

The external plot problems—both old ones from the old life and new ones from the new life—tear the lovers apart. Their internal conflicts also tear apart their relationship. All is lost and the relationship completely falls apart.

The hero/heroine's big gamble has utterly failed. The fresh start has gone terribly wrong, and now he or she can add having lost the love of his/her life to the list of failures, mistakes, and trauma.

THE END:

The lovers (separately or together) resolve the big problem(s) from the hero/heroine's past. The hero/heroine does not have to start again and can stay right here, where the love interest lives, and build a new life with him or her.

The hero/heroine finds a way to integrate the old life into the new life. It's a fresh start, but one that builds on the past and includes it as part of the hero/heroine's identity and life experience. The love interest knows everything he or she needs to know about the hero/heroine's past and loves him or her anyway.

The lovers build a life together that is, indeed, a fresh start for both of them in the wake of all the conflict and crisis they've successfully dealt with. Together, they have a clean slate and can move forward into the future together.

KEY SCENES

--hero/heroine arrives in the new place or in the new version of his/her life

--glimpse of the hero/heroine's past or at least a hint to the audience and love interest that something serious lurks in this person's past

--the person, problem, or threat from the past threatens the love interest

--the hero/heroine tries to leave this new life but stops or is stopped

--the hero/heroine tells all about his or her past to the love interest

--the hero/heroine and love interest make peace with the main character's past

. . .

THINGS TO THINK ABOUT WHEN WRITING THIS TROPE

What is the hero/heroine's past? Why is he/she walking away from it completely? What makes this the right decision for him or her? Is it, in fact, the right decision or not?

Does the hero/heroine walk away from the past before or after your story begins?

Does the hero/heroine assume a new identity entirely? A new name? New profession? A fake past?

Does the hero/heroine stay in his or her home, job, physical location, and relationships, but make a fresh start within this framework? If this is the case, how will the hero/heroine go about starting over? What does this do-over look like? How will he or she make it clear to everyone around him or her that he or she is making a fresh start?

Is your hero/heroine living partially, mostly, or completely off the grid? How will he or she pull this off?

How completely does the hero/heroine refuse to talk about the past with anyone? If he or she is surrounded by people who know about his or her past, how will he or she avoid facing it or dealing with it?

How do the hero/heroine and love interest meet? Or, if the love interest is someone out of the hero/heroine's past, when and how does he/she show up and how does the hero/heroine react?

What plot device will you use to throw the hero/heroine and love interest together repeatedly so they can get to know each other?

What person, problem, threat, crisis, etc. will follow the hero/heroine out of her or her past into this new life? How will that person or problem find the hero/heroine?

Is the love interest in danger from this past problem or person? If so, how much danger? What kind of danger?

How much trouble does the hero/heroine have trusting the love interest and vice versa?

What does the hero/heroine do to earn the love interest's trust? How does the hero/heroine prove himself or herself to be trustworthy?

What do friends and family of the love interest think of this mysterious stranger whom the love interest has fallen for?

Does the hero/heroine refuse to talk freely about the past? If so, why? How frustrated is the love interest that the hero/heroine refuses to talk about some or all of his/her past?

What does the love interest do behind the hero/heroine's back to try to learn more about the hero/heroine? What does he or she find out? Does the love interest confess to what they've learned to the hero/heroine? Why or why not?

What conflict, based on the external plot conflict of the story, threatens to tear apart the lovers? What internal disagreement(s) or conflict(s) threaten to tear them apart? How can you make these conflicts bigger, worse, or more wrenching?

At what point does the hero/heroine decide to leave and make yet another fresh start somewhere else? What or who stops him or her from following through on this decision?

What will the hero/heroine have to do to deal with the problem from his/her past? Can he or she deal with it alone or will he/she need the love interest's help to take care of it? Does he or she have to go back to his or her old life for a short time to fix the problem, or does the problem come to him or her in the new life?

At what point does the hero/heroine tell all to the love interest? What does the love interest think of it?

How does the hero/heroine heal from the wounds, trauma, and scars of his or her past? How does the love interest help with this healing process?

What does making peace with the past look like for both of these characters?

How will the couple integrate the hero/heroine's past into their future life together? Will they both walk away from the past together, or will they make it part of their life now?

How does the life the lovers build constitute a fresh start for both of them?

TROPE TRAPS

Creating a hero/heroine who's so secretive and inscrutable about their past that the audience dislikes him or her.

It looks like a cop out for the hero/heroine to just walk away from his or her past without dealing with the people, problems, and threats in his or her life. It turns off audiences to this character.

The hero/heroine never loosens up enough for the audience or the love interest to get to know him/her and like or love them.

The hero/heroine seems not very smart for having left a trail that people from his/her past could follow to find him or her.

The hero/heroine makes a big declaration of starting over but then continues to do all the same stuff that got him/her in trouble in the past.

The hero/heroine left behind a very serious problem that was bound to show up and put the new love interest in danger, and the hero/heroine should have recognized this. Instead, he or she selfishly fell in love and put the love interest in mortal danger, an action which isn't at all heroic.

The people in the new place or space around the hero/heroine blindly accept his or her story without asking any questions about who he or she really is. People are more cautious than that, in general.

The trauma in the hero/heroine's past isn't sufficient to have necessitated this reset of his/her entire life, which makes him or her look like a big ole' drama queen at best and a whiny baby at worst.

The hero/heroine looks paranoid for not trusting the love interest enough to tell him or her about the past as the two of them get to know each other.

The love interest seems naïve or stupid for falling in love with someone he or she knows nothing or very little about. This is a great way to end up dating a serial killer.

The problem that follows the hero/heroine out of the past is easy enough to resolve that the hero/heroine should have stuck around in his or her old life and just taken care of it instead of walking away and starting a new life.

Healing from the past is as easy as telling someone about it and deciding to move on from it. That's not how trauma works. It can take years of intensive therapy and personal growth work to move past a serious trauma, and the victim may never actually "heal" from it.

While it's a lovely sentiment to suggest that love heals all wounds, or that time heals all wounds, the reality is that love and time can help make wounds bearable but may never heal them. The trap here is naively suggesting to your audience that a trauma so serious a character up and left behind his or her entire life can be fixed simply by changing locations or meeting a new person.

If the hero/heroine has physically left their old life, failing to portray the difficulties of starting a whole new life—banking, mail, credit and credit cards, learning a new trade or profession, car registrations, passports, driver's licenses and other government identifications, phones, and more are a challenge to deal with.

FRESH START/DO-OVER TROPE IN ACTION
Movies:

- *Eat, Pray, Love*
- *Wild*
- *Under the Tuscan Sun*
- *Mom*
- *Jack Reacher (limited television series)*

Books:

- *Well Met* by Jen DeLuca
- *Beach Read* by Emily Henry
- *The Bride Test* by Helen Hoang
- *Silver Shark* by Ilona Andrews
- *The Golden Dynasty* by Kristen Ashley
- *The Widow of Rose House* by Diana Biller

19

GOODY TWO-SHOES

DEFINITION

The term Goody Two-shoes refers to someone who is extremely—possibly excessively—virtuous. It was popularized in an eighteenth-century fable that is a variation of the Cinderella story. Goody Two-Shoes is the nickname of a poor orphan girl named Margery Meanwell, who goes through life virtuously with only one shoe. When a rich gentleman gives her a complete pair, she is so happy that she tells everyone that she has "two shoes". Later, Margery becomes a teacher and marries a rich widower, and her virtue is rewarded.

Since then, the term has come to take on a more pejorative tone. The Goody Two-shoes can be someone so excessively virtuous they cross over into the realm of self-righteous and irritating to those around them. Although this term is traditionally applied to female characters, in recent times, it has become a unisex term.

This trope is the story of a hero or heroine who starts out as a (potentially unlovable) Goody Two-shoes and either changes and finds love or remains the same and finds someone who loves them as they are. He or she either finds someone who appreciates their virtue for the positive attribute it can be, or perhaps helps the Goody-Two shoes turn it into a positive virtue, or the Goody Two-shoes finally loosens up enough to be lovable.

Although not impossible, it may be difficult to create an appealing story between two Goody Two-shoes characters who meet, are attracted to each other, and fall in love. The odds of them both believing they've found their soulmate, immediately bonding, and never changing are very high ... and likely very boring to the audience.

The Goody Two-shoes trope is flexible in that the Goody Two-shoes hero or heroine may transform in this trope or may remain steadfast and unchanged. In either case, this is a trope of conflict between the core values and deeply held beliefs of your hero and heroine.

ADJACENT TROPES
--Shy Hero/Heroine
--Straight Arrow Seduced
--First Love
--Virgin Hero/Heroine

WHY READERS/VIEWERS LOVE THIS TROPE
--being worthy of and loved by your own knight/dame in shining armor
--being rescued by, or rescuing, the knight/dame in shining armor
--your own goodness and purity is seen and appreciated
--hero/heroine changes for you (or remains steadfast for you)
--introducing a naïve, inexperienced character to love

OBLIGATORY SCENES
THE BEGINNING:
The extreme goodness of the Goody Two-shoes character is

established. Often this is a scene of self-sacrifice or doing something to help another, possibly the future love interest, or witnessed by the love interest. It can also be a scene of the Goody Two-shoes character standing his or her ground in the face of a moral challenge.

The love interest is established as a more pragmatic character, perhaps more cynical, less good, or less perfect than the Goody Two-shoes. It's necessary to create a love interest for the Goody Two-shoes who will challenge his or her values or approach to life. Otherwise, you won't likely have much of a conflict to sustain your story.

The conflict between the hero and heroine's values is established.

THE MIDDLE:

The conflict between the hero and heroine's values unfolds. This is where the Goody Two-shoes is challenged to "loosen up." Regardless of whether this character's arc is one of steadfastness or change, the moral code of the Goody Two-shoes is tested and ultimately stretched to the breaking point.

The love interest of the Goody Two-shoes character examines and questions their own ethical and moral code. Are they good enough as is, or do they, too, need to change in some way?

The plot and/or the love interest lure the Goody Two-shoes into flirting with changing their rigid code of conduct. It may go seductively well, or it may go terribly. Either way, friction between the Goody Two-shoes and the love interest grows exponentially.

Will the Goody Two-shoes stand his or her ground, or will he/she change their ways? Indeed, the love interest likely experiences the same moral crisis. Should he or she clean up their act to meet the Goody Two-shoes where he or she is or hold fast as they are now?

BLACK MOMENT:

This can take several possible forms:

- The Goody Two-shoes just can't do it. He or she can't abandon his or her strongly held core beliefs/virtue.
- The love interest is devastated when he/she cannot rise to meet the impossibly high standards of the Goody Two-shoes.
- The Goody Two-shoes has "fallen" and blames the love interest.
- The love interest is guilt ridden when he or she successfully "corrupts" the Goody Two-shoes.

THE END:

Either the Goody Two-shoes has successfully loosened up and adopted a more realistic/pragmatic view of life, or he/she has success-fully withstood the challenge to their values and virtue. The love interest has either adapted to and accepted the rigid virtue of their Goody Two-shoes lover, or they have introduced the Goody Two-shoes to a whole new world of possibilities. Or these two have found a middle ground somewhere between the two opposite poles where they started the story.

In any case, the Goody Two-shoes and their love interest find common ground where they will be happy together.

A certain amount of caution is called for in any story where char-acters are forced to compromise their moral values. Better perhaps is the outcome where these two characters find core values they didn't know they had in common before the story occurred but that they can share going forward.

KEY SCENES

-- a "save the cat" scene taken to extremes (this refers to Blake Snyder's book, *Save the Cat*, wherein Snyder suggests that read-ers/viewers need to see the heroic main character act heroic right up front to establish sympathy and likability in the mind of the reader/viewer)

--the Goody Two-shoes refuses to budge in his or her values when the love interest really, really *needs* the Goody Two-shoes to budge

--the love interest feels unworthy

--temptation of the Goody Two-shoes

--the Goody Two-shoes gets beat up, literally or metaphorically, for standing his or her ground, and the love interest cleans up the Goody Two-shoes after the literal or metaphorical beating

--utter exasperation of the love interest

--the big fight as their values clash

THINGS TO THINK ABOUT WHEN WRITING THIS TROPE

When you start messing with changing a character's core values, you are treading on dangerous writing ground. It is very difficult to convince a reader that your main character is able, and furthermore willing, to change at such a deeply fundamental level. Indeed, peoples' core values are usually set in stone in childhood and rarely change after that.

If your Goody Two-shoes truly transforms in your story, what LIFE-CHANGING event occurs to justify such a radical shift?

Is your Goody Two-shoes going to transform in your story or remain steadfast in their virtuosity?

Is your love interest going to transform to be more like the Goody Two-shoes, remain the same in his or her core values, or meet the Goody Two-shoes somewhere in the middle?

How naïve or worldly are both your Goody Two-shoes and their love interest?

How has your Goody Two-shoes become this good? How were they raised as children to inculcate these powerful core values that stand up to all of life's temptations and challenges? Did they come by their values later as a result of some life-changing event? How do their core values look in practice?

Where does your Goody Two-shoes find the strength to stay the course?

What about your other main character does the Goody Two-shoes find irresistibly appealing?

What do these two characters have in common in their core values? (They probably must have some core values in common, or else they will never find a way to live together peaceably in the long run.)

Is your Goody Two-shoes truly this virtuous, or has their life experience taught them to act this way, well beyond the scope of their actual core values?

How does virtue manifest itself in your Goody Two-shoes? Are they loud and proud about it? Are they low-key about it? Secretive? Humble?

Does your Goody Two-shoes choose to do good quietly and anonymously, or are they performative in their goodness?

Is the Goody Two-shoes sincere or insincere in their excessive virtue?

How irritating is the Goody Two-shoes to those around them and to the love interest?

What does your Goody Two-shoes get from being this way? Praise? Notice? Self-affirmation? Self-esteem? A sense of doing right?

If your Goody Two-shoes ultimately changes, do they shatter all at once or change gradually, giving way in their values inch by agonizing inch?

Is the Goody Two-shoes compensating for some wrong done to them or by them in their past?

What about the Goody Two-shoes is attractive to the love interest?

What core values do the Goody Two-shoes and the love interest share?

How does the love interest feel about the relative perfection of the Goody two-shoes? Is it a source of conflict between them? What does that look like?

How bad does the Goody Two-shoes secretly yearn to be? Will they actually go that far in the story? How will the love interest seduce, tempt, or guide them to this "badness"? How does the Goody Two-shoes feel once they get there?

Does the Goody Two-shoes resent the love interest for trying to "corrupt" them or not? How guilty does the love interest feel about it?

TROPE TRAPS

Failure to justify why the Goody Two-shoes changed, if they change.

Creating a character so self-righteous that the reader hates them.

Creating a character who is so rigid in their values that they're unlikable. This rigidity can also make plotting very difficult. Where are the moral dilemmas, the mistakes, the false beliefs in a character who is utterly determined to stay exactly as they are and convinced they are absolutely right at all times?

Creating two main characters who are fundamentally so different in their core values that there's no realistic way they could ever fall in love.

The Goody Two-shoes seems weak for abandoning their morals.

The love interest seems craven, cruel, and unlikable for corrupting a "good" character.

The story doesn't create a compelling enough scenario for the Goody Two-shoes to change.

GOODY TWO-SHOES TROPE IN ACTION
Movies:

- *Captain America*
- *Blast from the Past*

- *Superman*
- *Easy A*
- *The Wizard of Oz*
- *Amélie*

Books:

- *Born of Fire* by Sherrilyn Kenyon
- *Twilight* by Stefanie Meyer
- *Outlander* by Diana Gabaldon
- *All the Queen's Men* by Linda Howard
- *The Best Man's Baby* by Victoria James
- *Eyes of Silver, Eyes of Gold* by Ellen O'Connell
- *Double Cross* by Carolyn Crane

20

HERO/HEROINE IN DISGUISE

DEFINITION

In this trope, the hero or heroine enters into a romantic relationship while in a disguise of some kind. The disguise can be a physical hiding of one's features, a hidden or false identity, or it can take the form of being undercover in some way, pretending to be someone the hero or heroine is not.

At some point, of course, the disguise will be revealed to the love interest and perhaps to the whole world. The hero or heroine's true self will be revealed. What effect will that have on the story, and more importantly, on the romance?

This is at its core a story of deception and its consequences and also a story of revelation of a hidden truth and its consequences. Both the form the deception takes and the truth that is ultimately revealed will shape not only the love story but its outcome.

ADJACENT TROPES

--Secret Identity
--Hero/Heroine in Hiding
--Disguised as a Male/Female

--On the Run/Chase

WHY READERS/VIEWERS LOVE THIS TROPE

--being in on the secret

--being able to see what others do not or cannot

--plain/common/humble love interest transforms into the enchanted prince/princess (or vice versa depending on the love interest's tastes)

--only you have the power to reveal the charming prince/princess

OBLIGATORY SCENES
THE BEGINNING:

The only requirement for this trope's beginning is that we establish for the reader that the hero or heroine is in disguise. Worth noting, in this story type the reader may know a secret that the love interest does not know. The love interest starts out as duped as everyone else in the story.

Also to be established for the reader: why the hero/heroine is in disguise.

THE MIDDLE:

As the story unfolds, we see the disguise in action. We see the love interest falling in love with the disguised hero or heroine, which throws the disguised character into conflict. If the disguised character reveals their true self, will they still be lovable? What if the love interest only loves the disguised version of them? How angry, sad, and disappointed will the love interest be if they discover the deception?

This is where the dangers of the hero/heroine's deception begin to reveal themselves.

It's possible the love interest meets the disguised hero/heroine as their true self out of disguise at some point in the story. This may or may not go well and may introduce a whole new set of complications for the disguised main character.

This may be (in terms of word count) where the first, mini black moment occurs—see below.

BLACK MOMENT:

This trope is unique in having not one, but two potential black moments. The first is when the hero/heroine reveals his or her true self—the real person behind the disguise—to the love interest. The second potential black moment is when the disguised character's disguise is unmasked for the whole world.

The former is potentially the *emotional* black moment of the story, and the latter is potentially the *plot* black moment of the story. These can happen in any order or at the same time but can be two entirely separate story beats. It's also possible that both of these reveals will have great emotional weight for the hero and heroine.

The usual rule of thumb is to put the most important emotional moments later in the story than the less important ones. Which is to say, most stories build toward a climax with the stakes rising in each successive scene toward the biggest emotional payoff.

Of course, the love interest and the whole world can find out about the disguise at the same time. Just be aware that two distinct emotional beats are occurring. Even in the case of a single, unified reveal to everyone, the most important emotional beat usually occurs last.

THE END:

The hero and heroine finally overcome the consequences of the deception—both the emotional toll and the plot complications. The love interest forgives the hero/heroine for their disguise, and they make a new start based in honesty between them. NOTE: It's not necessary that the hero/heroine in disguise ever reveal their hidden secret to the world for this couple to achieve their own private happily ever after.

KEY SCENES

--hero/heroine dons their disguise

--hero/heroine is almost caught (by the love interest or by someone else) out of disguise

--hero/heroine slips up and almost reveals the secret of their disguise

--love interest first suspects there's a disguise in play

--love interest sleuths for the truth

--love interest reacts to the big reveal of true identity

THINGS TO THINK ABOUT WHEN WRITING THIS TROPE

Why does the hero/heroine adopt a disguise?

What does that disguise look like, both physically, and in behavior?

Does the hero/heroine feel the same while in disguise, or do they feel like a different person?

Does the hero/heroine in disguise completely leave behind their original world to lose themselves in another, or do they move back and forth between their "real" world and their "pretend" world?

What does the love interest think of the hero/heroine in disguise? This could go one of two very different ways:

--the love interest may deeply dislike the hero/heroine's disguise. In turn, the disguised character may be convinced the love interest would be attracted to them if only they could show their true self

--the love interest may be deeply attracted to the disguised version of the hero/heroine, leaving the disguised character caught on the horns of a real dilemma. Should they abandon the attractive façade and risk losing the affection of the love interest, or should they try to maintain the disguise indefinitely?

Why does the disguised character eventually reveal his or her true self to the love interest? How does that reveal go?

How does the love interest feel about being deceived?

Does the disguised hero/heroine ever reveal their deception to the world at large? Why or why not? How does it go if he/she chooses to do it?

How much trouble is the disguised character in once his or her true identity is revealed? What kind of trouble? Legal trouble? Enemies coming for him or her? Family and friends furious?

Why does the love interest ultimately forgive the deception?

Does the love interest become part of the deception, or does the disguised hero/heroine ultimately join the love interest in the open, honest world?

What does the hero/heroine in disguise do to atone for their deception with the love interest?

TROPE TRAPS

The hero/heroine in disguise's dishonesty makes them unlikable to readers/viewers.

The love interest who doesn't see through the disguise comes across as stupid.

The reason for a character assuming a disguise is lame, or too weak to sustain the plot arc of an entire story.

The disguise itself is lame. The disguise needs to be believable enough that other characters in the story plausibly wouldn't see through it.

The consequences of the hero/heroine's deception, when revealed, aren't appropriate to the degree of deception perpetrated. Readers and viewers tend to have a highly developed sense of justice and generally want the punishment to fit the crime.

Readers or viewers fall in love with the disguise and are disappointed when the real character is revealed. Readers/viewers prefer the disguised version of the hero/heroine.

The love interest forgives the hero/heroine too easily for the deception.

Failure of the hero/heroine to tell the truth to their love interest sets up a fundamental disrespect for their partner.

HERO/HEROINE IN DISGUISE TROPE IN ACTION MOVIES:

- *The Scarlet Pimpernel*
- *Robin Hood*
- *Sister Act*
- *Man of Steel (or any Superman movie)*
- *Mrs. Doubtfire*
- *Mulan*
- *She's the Man*
- *Shakespeare in Love*

BOOKS:

- *A Rose in Winter* by Kathleen Woodiwiss
- *The Kingmaker Chronicles* by Amanda Bouchet
- *The Switch* by Lyndsey Sands
- *The Pathfinder's Way* by T.A. White
- *The Girl's Got Secrets* by Linda Kage
- *The Corinthian* by Georgette Heyer
- *Highland Rebel* by Judith James
- *Lament* by Maggie Stiefvater
- *Man of My Dreams* by Johanna Lindsey

21

MAKEOVER

DEFINITION

Before we discuss this trope, I must add a caveat: this is a trope to approach with care. The idea of making over a person can imply that her or she was somehow not acceptable or lovable before. In a world of body positivity, diversity, neurodiversity, inclusion, and embracing differences between us, it's vital not to create a character who wasn't wonderful exactly as they were before a physical makeover.

It's possible that this trope is not a physical makeover, but rather a life makeover. Again, I caution you to be very careful not to appear to negatively judge the before version of the character's life. That said, let's dive in.

This is, at first glance, a trope of external transformation. However, at its core, this is a trope of internal transformation. For the external transformation to be permanent, it must be a reflection of the deeper, more powerful, internal change.

In this trope, the hero or heroine reinvents himself or herself, or reinvents his or her life from the ground up, either alone or with help. Often the makeover encompasses both physical changes and lifestyle changes. The transformation is traditionally a dramatic one.

The traditional implication in this trope has been that this new version of the hero or heroine is now acceptable or attractive to the love interest, hence happily ever after follows on the heels of the makeover.

In point of fact, it's likely that the newfound self-love the made-over character finds is the catalyst to him or her finding true love. Which is to say, once the character loves himself or herself, he or she can allow for, believe, and/or accept the love that the love interest offers them.

Beware, beware, beware of the traps of this trope.

ADJACENT TROPES
--Ugly Duckling
--Plain Jane
--Fresh Start
--Running Away from Home

WHY READERS/VIEWERS LOVE THIS TROPE
--the idea of reinventing oneself from scratch
--uncovering the butterfly inside your very own caterpillar
--finding a perfect mate whom nobody else saw
--coming into sudden personal beauty is akin to coming into sudden wealth—you're swept away into a new, glamourous, and fabulous life

OBLIGATORY SCENES
THE BEGINNING:
We, and possibly the love interest, meet the "before" version of the hero/heroine and/or see the before version of her or her life. This is where you, the writer, will establish exactly what it is the hero/heroine is going to change about himself or herself over the course of the story.

Usually, the meeting between the main characters doesn't go well. Some fatal flaw in the untransformed hero/heroine and his or her life is demonstrated that makes a happily ever after with the love interest impossible.

Worth noting: it may be that the untransformed hero/heroine is perfectly acceptable as they are, but this character is too insecure, self-conscious, or lacking in self-esteem and confidence to pursue the love interest before undertaking a makeover.

Sometimes the big reveal of the made-over hero/heroine may happen at the end of the beginning, particularly if the makeover is merely a premise that sets up the main action of the story. Or the makeover itself may be the main action of the story, in which case, the reveal of the transformed hero/heroine will happen much later in the story.

THE MIDDLE:

The hero or heroine undertakes a makeover. This can be physical, emotional, a lifestyle or career change, or a combination of some or all of these, but it's a dramatic break with their past self to become a whole new person. The love interest may or may not be part of or privy to this transformation.

Take note of the fact that I didn't say the hero or heroine "undergoes" a makeover. In past versions of this trope, we often saw a character plopped into in a beauty salon chair, worked on by a team of experts, and voila, the hero or heroine emerges in a few hours completely stunning, and everything changes for the better in his or her life. In this version of the story, the hero or heroine is passive to the extent that they sit down and let somebody else do all the work.

I implore you not to ignore the real work of the makeover that has to happen inside the hero or heroine's heart and mind. He or she has a great deal of hard work to do to make the change permanent and come to terms with this new version of themselves. No matter how much external help the character gets to make the change happen, it's up to him or her to embrace it and sustain it.

The made-over hero/heroine begins to grapple with the changed life they have just been thrust into. This can go well or terribly, or both.

Regardless of whether the change happens gradually or all at once, the middle of the story often ends with the big reveal of the new self—perhaps to the love interest, or to the whole world, or both.

In a story where the big makeover reveal happens at the end of the beginning, the hero and heroine's relationship goes downhill through the middle of the book as they try and ultimately fail to come to terms with the makeover and its consequences, culminating in the black moment.

BLACK MOMENT:

The makeover has failed. Whatever goal the hero/heroine had in being made over is not achieved. The makeover was an utter failure. In this moment of crisis, the made-over hero/heroine must face the prospect of returning to their old self, old life, and all the old insecurities, doubts, fears, (and potential self-loathing ... but see the trope traps for this).

The love interest has failed to respond the way he or she was expected to and has let down the main character.

OR

The love interest feels completely betrayed or left behind by the hero/heroine's changes and walks away.

OR

The love interest sees that the changes the made-over character has made have either not changed the main character for the better or have changed him/her for the worse on the inside. The love interest calls the relationship quits.

THE END:

Obviously, the hero and heroine have some stuff to work out before this story can recover from the black moment. One or both of them engage in some introspection and honest self-assessment. One or both of them realize their mistake(s), see where they went off the rails in reacting to the makeover, and/or learn a major lesson. Not only do they each see their own mistakes, but they each take action to correct them.

This is probably where the made-over character finally internalizes the changes to himself/herself, and to his/her life and commits to sustaining the changes going forward.

This is also where the love interest finally makes peace with the changes to their partner, accepts them as real, and finally believes that the changed character isn't ever changing back.

Only then can the lovers reconcile.

The ship has been righted, its course reversed, and the failure leading to the black moment turned into a victory. The makeover has accomplished everything the hero/heroine hoped it would, and the makeover has succeeded after all.

OR

The hero/heroine never needed the makeover in the first place. He or she achieves their end goal and true love just as they originally were. Except now, he/she loves himself/herself and furthermore, the love interest also loves them as they are now.

The hero/heroine achieves their end goal(s) and finds true love—maybe just not the way they expected to.

· · ·

KEY SCENES

--moment of disappointment by the as yet not-transformed main character with his or her life or with how the first meeting with the future love interest went

--moment of humiliation for makeover character before the makeover. Although, that said, a moment of humiliation after the makeover would probably constitute a key scene in this trope, as well

--main character's decision to change

--big reveal of the makeover, particularly reactions of love interest and secondary characters

--regretting the change or missing the old self

THINGS TO THINK ABOUT WHEN WRITING THIS TROPE

What does the love interest think of the hero/heroine before the makeover? Does he or she notice the hero/heroine? Why or why not?

What kind of makeover will the hero/heroine undergo? Will this be a personal, physical makeover, a life makeover, or some combination of the two?

How arduous is it? How long will it take? How will you account for that time lapse in the story if it's a lengthy process?

Why does the hero/heroine want this makeover badly enough to go through the rigors of doing it? After all, if it were easy, this character likely would've done it before now.

How does the hero/heroine perceive himself or herself before the makeover? Does he/she like himself/herself? Does he/she have self-esteem problems, not see self accurately, perceive self as a failure when actually not one? Where is the disconnect between self-image and reality?

How will the main character address any emotional issues being played out in the form of a makeover? How will the love interest interfere with this and/or eventually help with this process?

Is there some non-self-esteem-related reason for this character to make over some aspect of their life that you can also use as your motivation for your hero/heroine to undergo a makeover?

What does the love interest think about the makeover itself? Does he/she think it's unnecessary? Support it anyway? Want to help? Find it ridiculous? Find it adorably silly?

What original, "before" aspects of the main character does the love interest fall for?

What new, "after" aspects of the main character does the love interest fall for?

What draws the hero/heroine to the love interest?

This trope tends to focus so heavily on the character doing the makeover that the love interest can get lost. What makes the love interest compelling, interesting, and engaging to the reader/viewer?

If there's a self-esteem issue in the main character, how does the love interest help the main character deal with that?

What does the love interest learn by watching the hero/heroine's makeover?

Does the love interest remain the same over the course of the story, or does he/she change in some way? How does the makeover help the love interest change or stay the same?

How will you show the changed character committing to and succeeding at maintaining the changes in self and lifestyle for the long term?

How will the changed character convince the love interest that the changes are real and permanent?

What does the changed character learn about himself/herself over the course of this transformation? How does it save or salvage the relationship?

TROPE TRAPS

Offending readers or viewers by suggesting the hero/heroine or their life NEEDS a makeover for any

reason, particularly if based on who they are to begin with or what their life is like.

Creating a hero/heroine who wants a dramatic makeover but doesn't really need one in the eyes of readers/viewers. This typically sets up an unlikable main character.

Creating a hero/heroine so crippled by self-esteem issues they're not emotionally healthy enough to find and maintain a healthy relationship with anyone else.

Creating a main character so needy that they're not likable or capable of a well-adjusted relationship with another person, makeover or not.

Creating a love interest who's unlikable enough up front (for not noticing or for ignoring the main character) that he/she can't be redeemed in the eyes of readers/viewers over the course of the story.

Just how shallow and unlikable is the love interest that they would be attracted to a made-over character but not the original version of this person?

Writer never acknowledging or dealing with the underlying emotional issues that cause a person to attempt a major makeover.

Hero/heroine (and love interest) not effectively dealing with the emotional issues inherent in a major makeover ... hence, sending a message to readers/viewers to ignore these issues and try to emulate the un-self-aware and/or self-destructive main character and love interest.

Sending a really negative message to readers/viewers about the type of person the main character is before their makeover, in effect declaring that the main character—and any reader/viewer who might happen to resemble that character—unlovable.

Not sufficiently developing the character arc from not loving self to loving self, and instead focusing solely on going from unlovable to lovable.

Creating a makeover that the main character isn't likely to sustain or doesn't have the resources to sustain for the long term.

• • •

MAKEOVER TROPE IN ACTION
Movies:

- *The Devil Wears Prada*
- *Mean Girls*
- *Clueless*
- *Pretty Woman*
- *The Princess Diaries*
- *Crazy Stupid Love*

Books:

- *Open Season* by Linda Howard
- *Making Faces* by Amy Harmon
- *Lock 'N' Load* by Tee O'Fallon
- *Melt For You* by J.T. Geissinger
- *The Matchmaker's Playbook* by Rachel Van Dyken
- *The Do-Over* by M.K. Schiller
- *Loving Cara* by Kristen Proby
- *See Jane Score* by Rachel Gibson
- *My Fake Rake* by Eva Leigh
- *You Don't Have to Say You Love Me* by Sarah Manning
- *A Reclusive Heart* by R. L Mathewson
- *Heaven, Texas* by Susan Elizabeth Phillips
- *Weightless* by Kandi Steiner
- *Beard Science* by Penny Reid

22

NERD/GEEK/GENIUS

DEFINITION

The hero/heroine is nerdy, a geek, or a genius. Which is to say, this hero/heroine doesn't fit in with regular society. Their love interest may not be any of these things, or may, in fact, be partially or totally the same. Inherent in this trope is the idea that the hero/heroine is "other" from society, and possibly from their love interest. Hence, I'm going to warn you to tread lightly with how you handle this trope. It's a perfectly fine trope with lots of possible story applications but may require extra sensitivity to handle the special attributes of the nerdy, geek, or brilliant hero/heroine.

At its core, this is a trope of a misfit searching for his or her place in the world, or of opposites attracting, or possibly of the love interest discovering their commonalities with the hero/heroine.

Worth noting: This is often a character type but not an actual trope in a story. The nerd/geek/genius becomes a trope when the hero/heroine's nerdiness/geekiness/genius becomes a major obstacle to love (or to the plot's outcome) and the conflicting worlds of the nerd/geek/genius and their love interest collide. Only then, does the characteristic of being a nerd, geek, or genius become the engine driving the story forward and suggest an inevitable beginning, middle, black moment, and ending.

ADJACENT TROPES
--Burdened by Beauty/Talent
--Socially Awkward Hero/Heroine
--Clumsy/Thoughtless/Bumbling
--Shy Hero/Heroine
--Opposites Attract

WHY READERS/VIEWERS LOVE THIS TROPE
--the misfit (which we all feel like sometimes) finds belonging and acceptance

-- being loved by the magical or special person

--entering a secret world (could be either the geeky world or the regular world)

--taming the beast, in this case not a violent one but possibly a clueless one, or at least bringing the beast into the real world

--he/she changes for you

--you know more or have more common sense than a super smart person

OBLIGATORY SCENES
THE BEGINNING:
The nerdiness, geekiness, and/or genius of the hero/heroine is established. The love interest reacts to these special attributes, usually not well. In most cases, it's established that the love interest is completely unfamiliar with the world the hero/heroine is immersed in, and vice versa. One or both characters is established as a misfit in the world of the other.

There are a few variations on this theme, depending on the nerdiness/geekiness/ and genius of the love interest. The love interest may be hiding their own similar attributes, or they may get an inkling that they have the same qualities. This similarity may make them run screaming, or it may cause an initial attraction to the nerdy/geeky/genius hero or heroine.

Often this is a comic trope. If so, right up front, hilarity should ensue as the oh-so-different love interest reacts to the extreme characteristics of the hero/heroine.

Conflict between their two worlds is established, but also attraction sparks.

THE MIDDLE:

Shenanigans and conflict ensue. This is where the love interest gets a deeper look into the nerdy/geeky/genius world of the hero or heroine. In the comic story, this is where the hero/heroine really gets their freak on and shows the love interest the true degree of their nerdiness, geekiness, or genius.

In the more serious story, this is where the love interest is deeply confused by, put off by, or just can't understand the world the nerdy hero/heroine inhabits. This "other" world may actually become dangerous for the "normal" character to navigate.

In the comic story, the misunderstandings get really ridiculous as both nerd/geek/genius and love interest let their true colors show.

Likewise, shenanigans and conflict ensue when the love interest introduces the nerd/geek/genius to the love interest's normal world. The nerd/geek/genius is a fish out of water and doesn't function any better in this world than the love interest does in the hero/heroine's world.

The differences between the partners become glaringly obvious, and the contrasts between their worlds sharpen. In the suspense version of this trope, the danger grows exponentially as each character navigates a totally unfamiliar world.

Conflict develops over which world this couple should inhabit for the long term if they're to end up together. The more their attraction and closeness grows, the larger this dilemma looms. Not only is this a conflict of physical surroundings, but also of which emotional universe to choose.

BLACK MOMENT:

The nerd/geek/genius and/or the love interest finally rejects their partner's world, rejecting the partner along with it.

The differences between the lovers are intractable and cannot be overcome.

The unfamiliar world each partner has tried to inhabit defeats them.

In despair, each partner returns to their own world, alone and devastated.

THE END:

Unable to find happiness alone, the partners realize they cannot live without the other and come back together. Now that they know how much worse it is to be apart than to make compromises or put up with the other's world, they're both willing to make sacrifices to find a way to be together.

The nerd/geek/genius is either accepted into their love interest's world, or vice versa. A variation on this: the lovers will each inhabit their own worlds when apart and will live in one world or the other when together. Or possibly, they create some compromise world somewhere in the middle between their different worlds.

The conflict between their worlds, or at least their relationships with their worlds, is resolved.

Any threats to one partner or the other from the opposing world are resolved.

· · ·

KEY SCENES

--the "normal" love interest laughs at the nerd/geek/genius or vice versa

--one or both characters get their feelings hurt

--moment of miscommunication that can be comic, tragic, or complicate the plot

--first foray into geek world by "normal" character

--nerd is unexpectedly great at romance or sex

THINGS TO THINK ABOUT WHEN WRITING THIS TROPE

What does the nerdiness, geekiness, or genius of the hero/heroine look like? Which character will be this way, or will both of them be this way?

If you choose for both characters to inhabit the nerd/geek/genius space, how will they be different from each other? After all, there's typically little to no conflict between nearly identical characters.

What does the "normalcy" of the love interest look like, and how does it manifest itself?

What about the "normal" world rejects or repulses the nerd/geek /genius? Why?

How did the nerd/geek/genius become the person they are? Why did they not learn to comfortably inhabit the normal world?

What is normal, anyway? Is there truly any such thing in your story? It's fine if there is. But it's worth the thought exercise of whether or not there is a real version of normal in your book's universe. Or is the love interest's world just as removed from "normal", but in a different way?)

What does each of these lovers find irresistible about the other? Why is it irresistible enough to give up the world they're comfortable in?

How hard is it going to be for each of these lovers to leave behind their known world for love? Why? What does this look like?

What force(s) make it nearly impossible for the nerd/geek-genius to fit in to the normal world? How will he/she overcome these obstacles? What does failure to overcome these obstacles look like? Can you make that outcome more disastrous?

How big a sacrifice is it for each of these lovers to leave behind their known world? Given that this is one of the biggest obstacles they have to overcome to achieve love, how can you make it an even bigger and more challenging obstacle to have to overcome?

TROPE TRAPS

Insensitively handling the differences of the nerd/geek/genius from others. Portraying the love interest's world as "normal" and the nerd/geek/genius's world as abnormal.

Creating too cliché a nerd/geek/genius. But this *is* a cliché by its very nature, you say. This trap can also be stated as creating a character that has no real, redeeming, human qualities, and portraying the nerd/geek/genius as a caricature.

The nerd/geek/genius and love interest have so little in common they couldn't possibly, believably, end up together in any universe. People with no core values in common rarely remain happy together for long, and all audience members know this.

Failing to have these lovers grow toward each other at least to some degree.

Failing to create a reasonable compromise between their worlds, their lives, and their outlooks on love.

Making fun too derisively of the world of the nerd/geek/genius— asking readers or viewers to laugh at the nerd/geek/genius instead of with him or her.

Portraying the nerd/geek/genius in such a way that readers or viewers wonder if this is actually a neurodivergent character whose characteristics are being insensitively portrayed or ridiculed.

Making the love interest mainly feel sorry for the nerd/geek/genius and making this the foundation of the romance. In most cases, pity isn't romantic.

NERD/GEEK/GENIUS TROPE IN ACTION
Movies:

- *Revenge of the Nerds*
- *A Beautiful Mind*
- *She's Out of My League*
- *Scott Pilgrim Against the World*
- *Good Will Hunting*
- *Crazy Stupid Love*
- *Eternal Sunshine of the Spotless Mind*

Books:

- *Dating-ish* by Penny Reid
- *Fangirl* by Rainbow Rowell
- *The Love Hypothesis* by Ali Hazelwood
- *Dark Wild Night* by Christina Lauren
- *Ready Player One* by Ernest Cline
- *The Kiss Quotient* by Helen Hoang
- *Nobody's Baby But Mine* by Susan Elizabeth Phillips

23

NEWCOMER/OUTSIDER/STRANGER

DEFINITION

Simply put, the hero or heroine is a newcomer to a place. This is one of those tropes that can be confusing because the quality of being a newcomer is not a trope in and of itself. The newcomer's newness, outsider-ness, or other-ness must be the driving force behind a conflict for it to rise to the level of being a trope. The "place" can be literal or metaphorical, but it's a space the newcomer must deal with, and which must deal with him or her.

Not all newcomers are good guys, of course, but in the context of a romance trope, the newcomer is almost without exception going to be one. This is a classic trope. The new sheriff who rides into town to clean up crime, the knight errant who arrives to vanquish the dragon, these are heroes of the newcomer trope.

Not only is the newcomer new to town, but he or she either has to change to adapt to the new place, or it has to change to adapt to them. This is where the newcomer becomes a fully developed story trope. It's about different worlds colliding.

Implicit in the newcomer trope is a conflict between opposing values that *must* be resolved ... or else. At its core, this trope often features star-crossed lovers, kept apart by families, traditions, cultures, taboos, etc. In its comic incarnation, this often takes the form of a comedy of misunderstandings.

Because a newcomer and a place do not generally constitute partners in a romance, there must be a love interest. The love interest may embody the values of the new place and this is where the conflict with the newcomer comes from. They may be an element of forbidden love to this relationship, or perhaps taboo love.

Or the love interest may be aligned in values with the newcomer but live in the place to which the newcomer has arrived. In this case, the newcomer and the love interest form an alliance to fight together against the opposing values of the place. The newcomer may rescue the love interest or may help the love interest rescue himself or herself.

ADJACENT TROPES
--Fish Out of Water/Cowboy in the City
--Across the Tracks
--Finding a Home
--Fresh Start
--Lone Wolf Tamed

WHY READERS/VIEWERS LOVE THIS TROPE
--swept away by a knight-in-shining-armor
--rescued from an impossible situation
--riding off into the sunset with your hero/heroine
--protected and taken care of
--the dark, dangerous stranger as hero
--the emotional drama of star-crossed lovers

OBLIGATORY SCENES
THE BEGINNING:

The newcomer arrives ... obviously. The newcomer's core values are established, and the love interest's values are also made clear. The world the newcomer is stepping into is established, as is the newcomer's conflict with it. The conflict can be one of behavior, values, ideas, property, cultures, families—sky's the limit. The love interest's relationship to the place is also laid out.

The foundation of conflict between the newcomer and the place and/or love interest is established. (Or the love interest's alliance with the newcomer is formed.) It's in this section of the story that the reader squarely lines up behind the newcomer, cheering for him or her as the definitive "good guy."

THE MIDDLE:

The conflict between the newcomer and the place he or she has come to becomes apparent. Conflicts between the newcomer and the love interest arise and also grow worse as the conflict with place intensifies.

Things go from bad to worse to terrible for both the newcomer, the new place, and the love interest. Whatever conflict you've chosen between the newcomer and the new world needs to cause escalating problems in the newcomer's relationship with the love interest.

BLACK MOMENT:

The newcomer is driven out. He or she has never fit in and never will. The newcomer leaves behind the love interest who is part of or tied to the place. These star-crossed lovers are never going to be able to overcome the obstacles standing between them, and all is lost. The newcomer's foray into this new place has failed, and along with it this couple's relationship has also failed.

THE END:

The newcomer returns, vanquishes the dragon—literally or metaphorically—and saves the love interest. The good people of the new place embrace the newcomer, and he or she is finally recognized as belonging in that place.

-OR-

The newcomer braves the dragon to rescue the love interest and leave the place behind. The dragon may or may not survive. The lovers (newcomer and love interest) ride off together into the sunset to find or make their own place in the world. In this scenario, the newcomer never changes or adapts to the new place. He or she comes, accomplishes a quest, rescues the love interest, and leaves, mostly unchanged. However, the place may be profoundly changed in the wake of the newcomer's visit.

KEY SCENES

--the newcomer doesn't fit in

--the newcomer truly sees the love interest when others do not

--love interest is ostracized for being friendly to or interested in the newcomer

--confrontation between newcomer and friends and family of the love interest

--newcomer and love interest are nearly caught or caught together

THINGS TO THINK ABOUT WHEN WRITING THIS TROPE

What kind of person is the newcomer and what are his or her core values?

What makes the newcomer likable and relatable, or at least recognizably heroic?

What place is he or she coming to? What are the core values of this place and how are they in conflict with the newcomer's values? In the serious drama, these may be heavy-duty values of good and evil, selfishness versus selflessness, greed versus charity, etc. In the comedy, these may be rather more light-hearted differences—cows are pets versus cows are hamburger on the hoof, sweat is icky versus the value of hard work, privacy versus nosy neighbors.

Does the love interest and his or her values align most closely with the newcomer or with the new place?

What is the main source of conflict between the newcomer and the love interest? What are some secondary conflicts between them that are loosely tied to the main conflict but somewhat different?

What will the conflict between the newcomer and the town look like?

What will the conflict between the newcomer and the love interest look like?

Do these two conflicts overlap? Are they the same? Are they completely different?

What does the newcomer have in common with the new place they've come to?

What does the newcomer already have in common with the love interest?

What makes the newcomer irresistibly attractive to the love interest and vice versa?

How do you plan to resolve your particular story? Does the newcomer stay or leave in the end? Does the place remain the same or changed in the end? Does the love interest remain the same or change by the end of the story?

How does the conflict between the newcomer and the new place resolve? Who wins? Who adapts and changes?

TROPE TRAPS

The newcomer fits in too easily or quickly, and there's not enough conflict to sustain a full story arc.

The conflict between newcomer and new place or love interest could realistically be resolved if everyone just sat down and had an adult conversation about it. That said, it's possible that there may be a realistic solution, but for one of many possible reasons, the bad guy, villain, or antagonist is unwilling to accept a reasonable solution.

The newcomer and love interest's core values are so different they would never plausibly end up together.

The newcomer and love interest have so much in common there's no conflict to make their relationship interesting or exciting.

The conflict with the new place is never satisfactorily resolved. Everyone just agrees to live with the core dissonance between them and pretend it doesn't exist. There's no real and lasting solution to the problem.

The newcomer sweeps into town, makes a bunch of changes but fails to slay the dragon, and then departs as abruptly as he or she arrived, leaving the people who remain behind in the place in the lurch—and potentially worse off than before because now they've got a pissed-off dragon in their midst.

Creating a wholly unsympathetic love interest.

Creating an emotionally unavailable loner as the newcomer who's not relatable or likable to readers or viewers.

NEWCOMER/OUTSIDER/STRANGER TROPE IN ACTION
Movies:

- *Divergent*
- *Hart of Dixie*
- *A Million Ways to Die in the West*
- *The Karate Kid*
- *Sweet Home Alabama*
- *The Moth Diaries*

Books:

- *Twilight* by Stefanie Meyer
- *Hush, Hush* by Becca Fitzpatrick
- *City of Bones* by Cassandra Claire
- *Flat-Out Love* by Jessica Park
- *It Happened One Summer* by Tessa Bailey
- *Drive Me Wild* by Melanie Harlow
- *Heart Bones* by Colleen Hoover
- *Archer's Voice* by Mia Sheridan

24

OBLIVIOUS TO LOVE/BELATED EPIPHANY

DEFINITION

As the title suggests, the hero or heroine in this romance is oblivious to love or doesn't realize he/she is in love with someone until too late in a belated epiphany. What constitutes too late, and with regard to what circumstance, is up to you, the writer.

The hero or heroine can exist in honest ignorance of potential romance swirling around him or her, or he/she can make an intentional choice to ignore romance. This typically serves as a source of frustration to the would-be romantic partner of the oblivious soul.

It's entirely possible that both the hero and heroine are simultaneously oblivious to love. In this scenario, one or both of them realizes too late that they were always in love, or should be in love, or are the right person to fall in love with going forward.

If the hero or heroine realizes too late that he/she loves someone, the question then becomes, what—if anything—will he/she do about it?

The oblivious partner takes a journey of growing awareness in this trope—becoming aware of the potential for romance already in front of him or her. The oblivious partner also takes an internal journey of learning to be aware of and receptive to love.

This is a transformation from closed heart and mind to open heart and mind for the oblivious character. In most oblivious-to-love stories, the epiphany by the clueless character comes too late, after they have apparently lost the person they finally realize they love.

This can a challenging trope to pull off if both partners in the romantic relationship are oblivious to love. If you want to write a doubly oblivious couple, you'll have to give particular consideration to how one or both of them finally breaks through the unawareness of romance potential between them.

This trope is often combined with tropes where the hero and heroine work, live, or are trapped in close proximity to each other. A few examples include: employee/boss romance, next door neighbors to happily ever after, childhood friends to lovers, and best friend's little sister/brother.

ADJACENT TROPES
--Clumsy/Thoughtless/Bumbling Hero or Heroine
--Nerdy/Geek/Genius
--Engaged to Someone Else
--Shy Hero/Heroine

WHY READERS/VIEWERS LOVE THIS TROPE
--catching the unattainable lover
--seeing what no one else saw (or being seen when no one else did)
--waking sleeping passion
--initiating an inexperienced lover
--having instant intimacy and a shared past with the one you love

OBLIGATORY SCENES
THE BEGINNING:

This trope absolutely requires that a platonic relationship be established between the hero and heroine to begin the story. In this relationship, (which may or may not be the result of another trope) the oblivious hero or heroine begins the story having no romantic interest in the future lover.

Two things must be established up front in this trope: first, that the oblivious character is completely unconscious of and unaware of the other character's romantic interest in them. Second, at least a hint of romantic interest must be established in the future love interest toward the oblivious hero/heroine. This romantic interest can be a tiny seed that will grow later, or it can be a spark, crush, or full-blown infatuation. Regardless of the degree of this romantic interest, the oblivious character doesn't see it in the beginning. At all.

THE MIDDLE:

The love interest tries and still fails to wake up the oblivious hero/heroine to the romantic possibilities between them. The frustration of the love interest is firmly established in the middle.

Also in the middle, the oblivious character may stubbornly refuse to see what's right in front of them, or the oblivious character may just be that unaware and not see the romance literally under his or her nose.

The end of the middle is usually defined by dawning awareness in the oblivious hero/heroine that more is going on than he or she was previously aware of. The lightbulb is starting to flicker on. The oblivious hero/heroine may still reject the idea of engaging in a romance, but he or she is probably starting to catch a clue.

BLACK MOMENT:

This trope is unique in that it may have two entirely separate black moments for each character in the relationship.

For the oblivious hero or heroine, the moment of realization that friendship, a work relationship, or some other platonic relationship has morphed into romantic love can be their black moment. This shift is likely disconcerting at best and devastating at worst. (Interestingly, this may actually be a moment of vast relief for the immensely frustrated love interest.)

As for the love interest's black moment, it potentially happens when he or she has made one last ditch effort to wake up the oblivious character to the love right in front of them, and the effort utterly failed or appeared to utterly fail.

Alternately, a black moment that occurs simultaneously for the oblivious hero/heroine and the love interest can happen when the oblivious hero or heroine, fully aware now that he/she and the love interest are WAY more than just friends, co-workers, neighbors, or the like, rejects love. This moment is equally devastating to both of them.

THE END:

The oblivious hero or heroine has finally wrapped his or her brain and heart around the idea of being in love. The love interest has forgiven the oblivious character for their denseness and also embraces the love he has seen as possible all along. The love interest is vindicated for believing in love first and rewarded for their perseverance and patience by finally getting their man or woman.

KEY SCENES

--the moment when the oblivious character becomes romantically aware of the love interest

--the love interest warned off (by a friend or loved one of the oblivious character, or by the oblivious character)

--the first romantic moment or love scene

--the return to obliviousness that crushes the love interest

•   •   •

THINGS TO THINK ABOUT WHEN WRITING THIS TROPE

Is the oblivious hero or heroine truly oblivious to love, or is he or she deliberately ignoring the possibility of finding love?

Why is the oblivious character that dense when it comes to seeing love and/or allowing himself/herself to give love a go?

Is the love interest also oblivious of love to some degree, too, or is the love interest completely aware of the romantic potential from the beginning?

What about the oblivious hero/heroine does the love interest find irresistible?

What does the oblivious hero/heroine find attractive/interesting/fascinating about the future love interest?

What is the source of the spark between these two characters? How will it be made clear on the page to readers or on the screen to viewers? Is it enough to sustain these characters' interest in each other and the reader's interest in their romance through the trials and tribulations of convincing the oblivious character to catch a clue?

Why is the potential love interest willing to stick around and wait for the oblivious character to get his or her act together? What about them gives them the patience/perseverance/stubbornness to hang in there with this frustrating person?

What and when is the first moment that it occurs to the oblivious character that there might be something romantic going on, here? How does he or she react to it? How does the love interest react to their reaction?

When did the love interest first find themselves romantically attracted to the oblivious hero/heroine? What did they do, or not do, about it back then? How do they feel now about what they did or didn't do?

How do the people around the hero and heroine feel about the idea of them having a romance? Do they support it, are they critical of it, do they interfere or matchmake?

Does the oblivious character keep their growing romantic interest secret from their potential romantic partner or not?

When in your story does the oblivious character fully recognize and admit to themselves that they're falling in love or already in love? Does this moment have the most dramatic impact in your story at this point, or should you move the moment somewhere else for maximum impact?

How does the love interest react when the oblivious character finally confesses to having romantic feelings for him or her? Is the love interest relieved? Ecstatic? Furious? Appalled? Why?

When, how, and why does the love interest forgive the oblivious character for their cluelessness?

What causes the oblivious character's view of the love interest to change? Is it a single significant event, or is it gradual—a series of small events that move the oblivious character by slow degrees?

What gambit(s) does the love interest try to show the oblivious character what they're missing that utterly fails? Why does it fail? Has the love interest miscalculated or does the oblivious character react unpredictably?

How do you want the reader to feel with the oblivious character finally wakes up to love? Which character in your story mirrors this feeling?

What's preventing friends, family, colleagues, or other secondary characters from simply pointing out to the oblivious character that the love interest is, in fact, interested in them? If they do point it out, why does the oblivious character ignore them?

TROPE TRAPS

Creating an oblivious character so dense as to be unlikable and unsympathetic.

Creating a love interest who has such low self-esteem that they're unlikable and unsympathetic.

Creating a completely unrealistic or unbelievable moment of

realization by the oblivious hero/heroine that there's romance in the air. This aha moment is critical to this trope. Screw it up and your story is ruined.

Creating one (or two) oblivious characters who would never realistically overcome their cluelessness to end up in love.

Failing to adequately address why the oblivious character is oblivious and failing to create sympathy for this character in the reader.

Failing to justify why the love interest is sticking around and waiting for the oblivious character to catch a clue.

Creating a situation where the reader is rooting for the love interest to just ditch the oblivious character and move on.

Rushing the discovery by the oblivious character of romance. Conversely, delaying the discovery artificially or too long can be equally frustrating to a reader.

Failing to explain why an otherwise intelligent, observant person could completely fail to notice love blossoming under his or her nose.

If there are secondary characters around this couple, failing to explain why one of them wouldn't smack the oblivious character upside the head metaphorically and point out the potential romantic interest they're ignoring.

Failing to adequately address how the love interest responds throughout the story. It's easy in this trope to get entirely caught up in the oblivious character's emotional journey and to ignore their partner's journey.

OBLIVIOUS TO LOVE/BELATED EPIPHANY TROPE IN ACTION
Movies:

- *My Fair lady*
- *Jerry Maguire*
- *Pretty Woman*

- *She's the Man*
- *Yesterday*
- *Love Actually*

Books:

- *The Thornbirds* by Colleen McCullough
- *Under One Roof* by Ali Hazelwood
- *The Language of Flowers* by Vanessa Diffenbaugh
- *Because of Miss Bridgerton* by Julia Quinn
- *The Winner's Curse* by Marie Rutkoski
- *Fire* by Kristen Cashore
- *Northhanger Abbey* by Jane Austen
- *Red Queen* by Victoria Aveyard
- *The Hunger Games* by Suzanne Collins

25

ONLY ONE NOT MARRIED

DEFINITION

This trope is about a hero or heroine who perceives himself or herself as the only one in some important group to them who is not married. This may, in fact, be true, or it may be a misperception. The group surrounding this character could be friends, family, work colleagues, or some other social grouping. The single character feels like a misfit in a world of people in long-term relationships, perhaps feels judged, and may feel lonely or even panicked.

The movement of this story centers around a character ultimately "fixing" this unmarried state and ending up married as well. In the historical world, not being married could have serious financial and social implications which made being unmarried a state worth panicking over. In the modern world, however, marriage is not necessarily perceived as the ultimate state of romantic bliss. Hence, creating a modern character desperate to end up married may require digging deeply into their personal motives for desiring marriage so desperately.

The internal journey of this character is movement from emotional pain to emotional fulfillment. This trope centers around a single character within your story. Therefore, it may be necessary to give the love interest of this eager-to-get-hitched character a trope of their own to describe their personal growth arc through the story. Also worth noting, authors often introduce an external (plot) obstacle to these two characters ending up together which may impede or prevent a wedding from happening.

ADJACENT TROPES
--Spinster/Bluestocking/On the Shelf
--Shy Hero or Heroine
--Ruined
--Socially Awkward Hero or Heroine

WHY READERS/VIEWERS LOVE THIS TROPE
--getting your own fairy tale ending
--achieving true love and happily ever after
--not being alone or lonely any more
--receiving a great gift (a proposal, a ring, a wedding)

OBLIGATORY SCENES
THE BEGINNING:
The main character is established as being single, while at the same time, everyone around him or her is established to be married or in stable, happy, long-term relationships. The main character's envy, panic, fear, loneliness, etc. is established, as is their desire to change their single state. The social group around the main character is introduced. The potential love interest is introduced. The main character's decision and/or resolve to get married is shown.

Since this is a trope very likely to be layered with another trope, the secondary trope is also introduced. Worth noting: the first major single character of the gender appropriate to be a love interest to your main character is likely to be the one readers or viewers expect the single character to end up married to. If this is not the case, be careful to signal that to your audience.

THE MIDDLE:

The single character's pursuit of love progresses. If the main character is pursuing one person through the story, the middle will be filled with the ups and downs of dating and romance. If the single character is sorting through multiple possible love interests, the middle will be filled with a variety of disasters and disappointments.

Toward the end of the middle, our unmarried character may have zeroed in on a single potential mate and be pursuing them single-mindedly. As the book progresses, the romance between these two will also progress. But, because this is a romance novel, some insurmountable obstacle is looming in the distance and coming closer with every page turned.

BLACK MOMENT:

All of the unmarried character's plans to end up married fall apart. The insurmountable obstacle inside the main character or the love interest's doubts explode, and the wedding or engagement is called off.

If there is one, the external obstacle proves too much to overcome and the wedding is blocked or stopped.

If a plot device is used to stop the wedding, be sure not to rely solely on it. Doing this is usually considered lazy writing by readers and viewers. Don't rely on a *deus ex machina* (an act of God) to get around there not being another, stronger, emotional reason for the wedding not to happen. One or both of the main characters should also have strong internal reasons that prevent the wedding from going forward.

. . .

THE END:

The obstacles, internal and external, are finally cleared and the engagement or wedding happens. The formerly single character finally is happily married and fits in with everyone around them now. Not only do they have love, but their entire life is better now.

THINGS TO THINK ABOUT WHEN WRITING THIS TROPE

Why is the unmarried character still single?

Why is it so important to this character to get married? What do they expect to get out of it? How do they expect to feel once they get married?

Who is the love interest? Is he or she worthy of the search the unmarried character has gone through to find them?

What peer group around the unmarried character is the standard by which he or she is measuring himself or herself?

Why is the main character so desperate to fit into this peer group?

How does the main character feel about not being married? What secondary emotions are they also feeling about their unmarried state?

Is there some external, plot reason that these two people should not get married? For example, a policy that two people in the same office may not date or marry, or the terms of a will prevent the desperately single character from marrying before they inherit. There are any number of external forces or reasons that would stop two people from being able to marry. Some of them may be tropes unto themselves, some may be plots or plot devices.

What is the emotional journey this character takes over the course of pursuing marriage? Where does it start? Where does it end?

Does anyone around this character try to set them up with a suitor? How does that go?

How do the secondary characters around this single person relate to him or her with regard to their single state?

How eager or reluctant is the love interest to get married in the beginning?

How hard does the single character have to work to convince their partner to get married? How does he or she feel about that?

At some point in the story, does the single character find the means, self-confidence, self-esteem, etc. to be okay with remaining single?

In the end, does getting engaged or married live up to his or her expectations? In what way(s) is it different and better than he or she expected?

TROPE TRAPS

Creating a character who's so desperate they come across as pathetic or pitiful.

Modern audiences being unable to relate to the single character's desperation to find love.

Creating a story so dynamic where the eager-to-be-married character steamrolls or bullies their love interest into marriage.

Failing to convincingly justify why this character wants and/or needs so much to be married.

Focusing too much on marriage as the end goal instead of love, respect, companionship, and happiness as the end goals.

The main character cynically pursuing marriage for the wrong reasons and never realizing why one should actually enter into marriage.

Equating love and marriage as being the same thing. Equating safety and marriage as the same thing.

ONLY ONE NOT MARRIED IN ACTION
Movies:

- *My Big Fat Greek Wedding*

- *My Best Friend's Wedding*
- *Princess Diaries 2*
- *Four Weddings and a Funeral*
- *The Wedding Date*

Books:

- *Always* the Bridesmaid by Lindsey Kelk
- *Murder with Peacocks* by Donna Andrews
- *Persuasion* by Jane Austen
- *Devil in Winter* by Lisa Kleypas
- *Nine Rules to Break When Romancing a Rake* by Sarah MacLean
- *Any Duchess Will Do* by Tessa Dare

26

PLAIN JANE/JOHN

DEFINITION

One might ask why this trope is contained in a book about internal tropes. While physical plainness is an external feature, the act of feeling plain, presenting oneself as plain, and relating to others as if unremarkable or unattractive is most certainly an internal issue. In reality, every person has plenty of attractive features, if not physical, certainly emotional, social, intellectual, and other intangible features.

This trope is technically about a "plain" person finding love. But, at the end of the day, it's really not their physical plainness preventing him or her from finding love. It's their own perception of self as plain or even unlovable that is the obstacle which must be overcome in order to find happily ever after.

This is NOT a makeover trope. Jane/John's plainness doesn't change in this trope. Jane/John and the love interest merely learn to love both the plain and beautiful quality(ies) that Jane/John has.

This trope is a journey of finding self-love, thereby making loving someone else and being loved by another person possible.

· · ·

ADJACENT TROPES
--Makeover
--Ugly Duckling
--Spinster/Bluestocking/On the Shelf
--Straight Arrow Seduced

WHY READERS/VIEWERS LOVE THIS TROPE
--who doesn't relate to a character who feels inadequate, unattractive, or plain in some way?

--a Cinderella transformation in your heart

--going from being seen as plain to being seen as beautiful just as you are

--going from unlovable to lovable

--being accepted just as you are

OBLIGATORY SCENES
THE BEGINNING:
We meet the Jane or John and we see how they, and possibly others, perceive them to be. How Jane or John feels about their plainness is established. We meet the potential love interest, and we see this person overlook or underestimate Jane or John. Circumstances in the story throw the Plain Jane/John and the future love interest together.

THE MIDDLE:
Jane/John's plainness gets in the way of love. Jane or John may be desperately pursuing love and struggling to overcome their perceived shortcomings. Or the love interest may be struggling to convince Jane/John that he or she is, in fact, lovable. Or the story elements may be the only thing holding these two people together until they gradu-

ally start getting to know each other and begin to find redeeming qualities in each other.

While there are likely to be other story elements getting in the way of our lovers finding their happily ever after, Jane or John's self-image (or the perception of them by their potential love interest) comes to the fore as an obstacle to love.

BLACK MOMENT:

Either Jane/John or the love interest decides the relationship is doomed and cannot continue. All is lost for Jane/John, and he or she knows it's because of their plainness and unlovability. Jane/John is devastated and bereft. (And very likely, the love interest is also bereft.)

THE END:

Jane/John finally overcomes his or her negative self-image and learns to see himself/herself as beautiful in their own way and worthy of love. The love interest, likewise, finally sees the ultimately lovable, "beautiful" qualities in Jane/John and falls fully in love with Jane or John. Typically, Jane/John must forgive the love interest for being blind all this time, or conversely, Jane/John must apologize for being stubbornly unable to see their own best qualities until now. This true love is all the sweeter for being based on the qualities that make a person genuinely lovable.

KEY SCENES

--the first time Plain Jane/John sees the unattainable love interest
--the first time the love interest notices Plain Jane/John.
--their first romantic moment
--declaration by the love interest that Jane/John is beautiful

--the moment when Jane/John finally sees self as attractive, lovable, and beautiful

THINGS TO THINK ABOUT WHEN WRITING THIS TROPE

What form does John/John's plainness take? Is it physical? A quality of temperament? A personality trait?

Is the plainness real? Or is it partially or completely in the mind of Jane/John?

How does Jane/John feel about herself/himself? Do they like themselves or not? Are they at peace with their plain quality(ies) or not?

Why does Jane/John believe herself or himself not to be lovable? What event(s) in the past have taught them this lesson?

What about Plain Jane/John is pure, beautiful, and breathtakingly lovable? How will you show this to readers, viewers, and to the other characters in the story?

How does the love interest initially perceive Jane/John? Does he/she see Jane/John the same way Jane/John does, or does he/she see someone entirely different?

What's the tone of their first meeting? Is it a comic meet-cute? Of no great importance to the love interest but devastating to Jane/John? This scene and the character's perceptions of it will set the tone for the entire story.

How does Jane/John feel about how the love interest perceives them initially?

What changes the love interest's perception of Jane/John as being plain? Is it a single big realization, or is it a gradual series of small realizations?

What does the love interest think of Jane/John's perception of self?

When and how does Jane/John's perception of self-change?

Is the love interest the one who changes Jane/John's self-perception, or does Jane/John ultimately change their own self-perception?

How is the love interest changed by the journey of loving Jane/John? What life lessons does the love interest learn from this relationship?

What does happily ever after look like for these two people?

How do the people around this couple ultimately react to Jane/John and the love interest finding true love? Are the secondary characters changed as well, or do they remain the same in their beliefs, for better or worse?

When does the power dynamic between Jane/John and the love interest switch in the story? At some point, it must change from Jane/John as supplicant to Jane/John as the more pure, more worthy, more self-aware character in the relationship. Usually this happens near the end, but usually, the love interest has to come back to Jane/John as a supplicant.

TROPE TRAPS

Beware of creating pity for Plain Jane/John—both in secondary characters and in your audience.

Creating a character who's unlikable and has no redeeming qualities. It's fine for characters not to be movie-star gorgeous, but it's not fine for them to be thoroughly awful people.

Giving in to the impulse to do a makeover on this character, particularly so the love interest can finally see them as beautiful. This creates a shallow love interest not worthy of true love.

Failing to justify why Plain Jane/John sees themselves as unlovable in the first place. This is a profound (and tragic) self-understanding, and it has to come from somewhere.

Creating a love interest without the emotional and intellectual depth to see past the surface of Plain Jane/John.

Creating a love interest who sees too easily or quickly past the plain façade. This is a major source of conflict for your story. Don't rush it.

Failing to create a series of interactions where Plain Jane/John shows the love interest their best, most lovable qualities.

Creating a love interest who's ultimately not worthy of Plain Jane/John.

PLAIN JANE/JOHN IN ACTION
Movies:

- *Washington Square*
- *Plain Jane*
- *That Model From Paris*
- *The Taming of the Shrew*
- *Sense and Sensibility*
- *From Miyamoto to You*

Books:

- *Sarah Plain and Tall* by Patricia MacLachlan
- *Heaven, Texas* by Susan Elizabeth Phillips
- *Lover Eternal* by J.R. Ward
- *Never a Gentleman* by Eileen Dreyer
- *The Duke and I* by Julia Quinn
- *The Ugly Duchess* by Eloisa James
- *The Raven Prince* by Elizabeth Hoyt

27

PLUS SIZE LOVE

DEFINITION

In this trope, either the hero or heroine is a plus-sized character, and the story revolves around their body shape and self-image. Traditionally, the heroine is the curvy character, but either is possible. It's entirely possible to write a plus-sized character and NOT have this be a trope, but merely a physical characteristic that is simply the way a character looks.

For plus-sized love to become a trope in a story, how that character and their love interest relate to his or her body must become an important part of the story and lead to plot and story developments.

This is NOT a story of physical transformation. In this trope, the plus-sized character remains plus-sized throughout the story. It likely IS a story of internal transformation, one of learning to love self as is and becoming accepted as is. This transformation can be a solitary journey that the plus-sized character makes on their own in the story, in which case, the love interest will likely need a trope of their own to wrestle with over the course of the story. Or if the plus-sized character enlists the love interest in their journey of transformation, this trope can sustain a complete story arc for both main characters.

Sometimes, the fact of being plus-sized is not the actual self-esteem issue this character is wrestling with. Instead of being the actual problem, physical appearance can be a stand-in for some other deeper, hidden trauma that this character must deal with. I bring this up because this trope can easily slip into being a very superficial and even distasteful trope to readers/viewers if not handled with loving care.

One way to prevent that is to insert a secondary (or actually primary) trauma into the life of the plus-sized character, thereby creating a more layered and nuanced character who doesn't rely purely on a physical characteristic for conflict, growth, or an obstacle to love to be overcome.

ADJACENT TROPES
--Right Under Your Nose
--Plain Jane/John
--Ugly Duckling

WHY READERS/VIEWERS LOVE THIS TROPE
--most people, rightly or wrongly, wish to be smaller, so they may find a self-conscious character extremely relatable
--embracing the voluptuous body as god- or goddess-figure
--embracing sensuality in all its forms
--in reality, everyone is attractive
--finding the one perfect person who adores you exactly as you are.

OBLIGATORY SCENES
THE BEGINNING:
The plus-sized main character and their future love interest meet. Both of them have opinions and reactions of some kind to the body-type of the plus-sized character. This trope has limitless options: the

plus-sized character loves his or her own body, hates his or her own body, is completely at ease in his or her skin, or is deeply uncomfortable in his or her skin. The love interest can react with any degree of attraction or lack of initial attraction. That said, a spark must be established between these two characters which will move forward into the middle of the story and grow or be challenged. Whether it's a spark of friction or nascent attraction is up to you.

THE MIDDLE:

The ebb and flow of a developing romance happens, with the body-type and shape of the plus-sized character front and center in either that character's mind and/or the love interest's mind. This character's body type either becomes an obstacle to their love, or it becomes an attraction that pulls two otherwise unlikely lovers together. And yes, it can do both in the same story.

The plus-sized character wrestles with his or her appearance, and/or the love interest wrestles with it. The reason why one or both of them struggles with it and what form that struggle takes is up to you.

BLACK MOMENT:

The plus-sized character's aspirations of finding true love fail catastrophically. Either the plus-sized character or the love interest or both blame the plus-sized character's appearance for a break-up that possibly has nothing whatsoever to do with that, at its core.

THE END:

Both the underlying, core problem with the relationship and both lovers' relationships with body image are resolved. This clears the way for true love, and your plus-sized hero or heroine and their true love finally find their happily ever after.

. . .

KEY SCENES

--the moment of first sight, which will set the tone for the entire story

--the first time the plus-sized character gets naked (literally or metaphorically) in front of the love interest

--the first (or perhaps only) conversation about body image

THINGS TO THINK ABOUT WHEN WRITING THIS TROPE

What does plus-sized look like in these characters' worlds?

How does the plus-sized character feel about their body type and body image? Now, how does he/she *really* feel about it? I'm not trying to intimate that all plus-sized characters must feel bad about their bodies. Far from it. I'm merely pointing out that there are the feelings we acknowledge to ourselves and the deeper, hidden ones we often don't acknowledge to ourselves.

Why does the plus-sized character feel this way about himself or herself? When did these feelings begin? When did they change from something else to this?

Does the plus-sized character try to hide his or her body, or is he/she out and proud about his or her appearance?

If the plus-sized character's size is a problem for them, is it the actual problem in and of itself, or does it mask some deeper trauma that may be hidden from others and/or hidden from this character himself or herself?

If that hidden trauma exists, what is it? When did it happen? What life-altering lessons did the plus-sized character take away from that trauma? How did it change this character's self-image and way of interacting with the world?

Did the trauma cause a change in physical appearance? If so, why?

If the plus-sized character is carrying around a deeper trauma, how will it be revealed in the story, and how will it be resolved?

Why is the love interest the right person to stand beside the plus-sized character as they deal with past trauma and/or self-image issues?

How do the plus-sized character and the love interest meet? What are their first impressions of each other? How accurate or wildly inaccurate are those first impressions?

Specifically, how does the love interest feel about the plus-sized character's appearance? Why does the love interest feel this way?

Does the plus-sized character believe the love interest when he or she expresses his or her feelings about the plus-sized character's appearance?

What elements of your story will help the plus-sized character come to terms with their plus-ness? What elements of your story will hinder this character from coming to terms with their own physical appearance?

How do the secondary characters perceive the plus-sized character? Do they help the romance along or try to hinder it? Why?

What lesson(s) do both the plus-sized character and love interest learn over the course of this story regarding physical appearance?

What is the core basis of love between these two characters that goes entirely beyond how either of them looks? How will these two characters discover that core love? What stands in the way of them seeing each other as they truly are?

TROPE TRAPS

Focusing solely on how the plus-sized character looks and coming across as shallow and superficial.

Offending readers or viewers by judging a character by his or her exterior only.

Creating a deeply unlikable love interest because he or she can't see past the surface of a person's appearance to find the truly lovable person beneath.

Failing to create an actual trope arc when including a plus-sized character in your story. It's absolutely fine (and awesome, in fact) to write characters who are not all living embodiments of Barbie dolls.

Failing to create a compelling emotional arc regarding how the plus-sized character relates to his or her physical appearance.

Creating a shallow main character who is only concerned about how they look.

Failing to develop lovable, wonderful qualities in the main character in addition to their voluptuous physical attributes. Again, I'm not trying to say this character cannot be loved for being voluptuous. I'm merely saying that judging any person's worth solely on how they look is a recipe for romantic disaster in the minds of audiences.

Failing to recognize or address the deeper trauma that has nothing to do with physical appearance, but which is masked by a plus-sized character's physical appearance.

PLUS SIZE LOVE IN ACTION
Movies:

- *Isn't It Romantic?*
- *Hairspray*
- *Holiday*
- *Phat Girlz*
- *Sierra Burgess Is a Loser*
- *Fatso*
- *Shallow Hal*

Books:

- *The Ugly Girlfriend* by Latrivia S. Nelson
- *Get A Life, Chloe Brown* by Talia Hibbert
- *One to Watch* by Kate Stayman
- *Perfection* by R. L. Mathewson
- *Dipped in Holly* by Dana Isaly
- *Bet Me* by Jennifer Crusie
- *Spoiler Alert* by Olivia Dade

28

REBELLIOUS HERO/HEROINE

DEFINITION

Ahh, who doesn't love a good rebel in a love story? This rebel is not to be confused with a bad boy or bad girl, however. The rebellious hero or heroine is legitimately rebelling against something they disagree with—a societal norm, a family requirement or prohibition, a belief, a teaching, or something else that he or she refuses to accept as an obstacle to love.

Generally, in the romance space, the thing the hero or heroine is rebelling against is preventing him or her from achieving true love. In some cases within romance and frequently outside of romance, the rebellion will be against some other factor that limits the personal freedom of the hero or heroine.

The rebel may succeed in bucking the norms being rebelled against, or this person may eventually come to understand the reasons for the norm they initially refuse to follow. In either case, love wins in the end, of course.

This is one of those tropes that could sit in the category of external tropes as easily as it sits in the internal trope category. What makes this an internal trope is the transformation of one or both of the main characters over the course of facing this challenge. Their internal beliefs, decisions, or understandings change over the course of the story. As an external trope, the person, idea, norm, rule, or system impeding the love story ends up being changed. In reality, you may choose to do both in your story.

ADJACENT TROPES
--Bad Boy/Girl Reformed
--Lone Wolf Tamed
--Hero/Heroine is Ex-Con
--Redemption

WHY READERS/VIEWERS LOVE THIS TROPE
--this character has the courage the reader wishes he or she has

--the good guy wins in the end. Justice, Right, and Fairness are served.

--who doesn't fantasize about breaking the rules or telling off the Man?

--the rebel says aloud all the things we wish we were smart enough to think of and brave enough to say

--the rebel is a knight in shining armor, sweeping away the beleaguered love interest out of their oppression, misery, and unhappiness. Gimme some of that!

OBLIGATORY SCENES
THE BEGINNING:
The person, thing, idea, or norm the rebel is rebelling against is established, and how this is interfering with achieving the rebel's goal is shown. Traditionally in a romance, the rebel seeks love, which is forbidden.

But the rebel can certainly be rebelling against something or someone over some other cause. If this is the case, that cause should probably be negatively affecting the love interest, as well. Otherwise, the cause in the story may threaten to overwhelm the love story and instead become a social treatise. Which is to say, in the romance space, choose your cause with an eye to keeping the focus of your story on the romantic couple.

THE MIDDLE:

The complications separating this couple mount. The system strikes back, and the danger increases with every passing page as the hero and/or heroine fight the system. I say and/or because it's possible the love interest is not actively rebelling against whatever the rebellious hero/heroine is. The love interest may be increasingly panicked at the rebel's choices through the middle of the story as the risks become almost too much to stand.

If there's a good reason for the system being the way it is, this is where that argument will get made. The middle of this type of story is all about doubts, conflict between hero and heroine over the rebellion they're undertaking, small victories, and larger setbacks.

BLACK MOMENT:

The rebellion has failed. All is lost, and the price is loss of love. The lovers are torn apart and that which they've been rebelling against appears to have won.

THE END:

In a stunning reversal, usually requiring great courage and willingness to sacrifice everything, up to and including life and limb, the rebellious hero/heroine and the love interest triumph over the thing they're opposing and which has been keeping them apart. The lovers are reunited at last. At great cost and risk, they've finally achieved their triumph over their opposition and earn their happily ever after as a reward.

KEY SCENES

--the scene establishing just how bad a person/thing/rule/system the rebellious hero/heroine is up against is

--the first forbidden kiss or love scene

--nearly getting caught being together

--getting caught being together

--the consequences of being together are established

THINGS TO THINK ABOUT WHEN WRITING THIS TROPE

What exactly is the rebellious hero/heroine rebelling against? How does this thing interfere with or prohibit the relationship this character would like to have?

What is the relationship of the love interest to the thing or person the rebel is fighting? Is the love interest part of the system being rebelled against? A relative or loved one of the person being rebelled against? An enforcer of the rule being rebelled against?

How is the love interest a victim of the thing or person being rebelled against? Is the love interest aware of this in the beginning? If not, when does the love interest become aware of it?

How will the love interest rebel against the person or thing the rebel is fighting against?

Will the love interest try to talk the rebel out of their crusade? Doubt the rebel? Fully embrace the rebel's cause? Consider betraying the rebel? Be coerced into betraying the rebel?

Where do the love interests loyalties lie in the beginning, middle, and end of this story? How do they change over the course of the story? What changes those loyalties or causes them to remain steadfast?

Is the person or thing being rebelled against ultimately good or bad? Does the rebellious character come around to understanding why the person or thing is as it is, or does the rebel ultimately decide the person or thing is bad and must be taken down?

How bad is your bad guy? Keeping in mind the badness of your bad guy determines the goodness of your good guy. How can you make the bad guy much, much badder?

Perhaps the most important element of this entire story will be how the rebel and their lover turn the tide in the climax of the story and defeat the bad guy, after the bad guy has appeared to resoundingly win. Even for a pantsing writer, it's worth figuring out how the good guys (the lovers) will overcome the bad guy(s) in the end well before you start drafting this story. This is almost guaranteed to be the plot point that stumps you in creating this type of story.

When considering this plot point, ask yourself:

--how much are the rebel and the love interest willing to sacrifice to defeat the bad guy?

--if the rebel and love interest are willing to die to win, why are they willing NOT to end up with the person they love in the end?

--is the intent for the rebel and lover to die together or to survive together? Does your big climax take this into account as the lovers plan their final attack?

--is one of the lovers more willing to die to save the other? How does this imbalance affect their relationship? Is there a good reason for this imbalance?

--how clever, lucky, or skilled does the rebel have to be to win? What form will this take, that is, how will he or she pull off what seems impossible?

TROPE TRAPS

The rebellious hero/heroine and their love interest simply don't plausibly have the resources or skill to defeat the person or thing they're taking on.

The big confrontation at the end where the lovers' fortunes are reversed, victory is snatched from the jaws of defeat, and they finally win isn't believable. At all. I put this one in bold letters, as it's by far the most common fatal flaw I see in the execution of this trope.

Shortchanging the reader of a satisfying final confrontation—not making it big enough, dangerous enough, or clever enough to fit the badness of the bad guy.

Rushing the big confrontation.

Choosing a cause for the hero or heroine to rebel against that readers/viewers don't care about or find compelling.

Hitting the reader or viewer over the head with a political, social, or societal cause sledgehammer. Audiences HATE this. They signed up to be entertained, not get lectured.

Even if the love story using this trope is a subplot in another genre of fiction, readers and viewers still HATE being lectured.

Creating too weak, whiny, or spineless a love interest to stand beside this courageous rebel as a plausible partner. It's worth noting that courage can take many forms. It doesn't always have to be in-your-face brashness. The love interest can be subtle in their resistance to the thing the rebel is openly fighting against.

Talking the rebel out of their cause with a lame argument or with an explanation of why something is the way it is that is so obvious the rebel should have seen it before.

Creating a rebellious hero/heroine who's merely angry and not actually justified in their outrage.

REBELLIOUS HERO/HEROINE IN ACTION

MOVIES:

- *Footloose*

- *Hunger Games*
- *Dirty Dancing*
- *Mulan*
- *Tootsie*
- *The Breakfast Club*
- NOTE: There are many movies that feature rebellious heroes/heroines that don't end with a happily ever after. They are nonetheless good studies of how this trope works. They include *Gone with the Wind, Doctor Zhivago, Last of the Mohicans, Romeo and Juliet,* the *Star Wars* movies, and more.

BOOKS:

- *The Prize* by Julie Garwood
- *Hunger Games* by Suzanne Collins
- *It's In His Kiss* by Julia Quinn
- *Never Love a Highlander* by Maya Banks
- *Divergent* by Veronica Roth
- *An Ember in the Ashes* by Sabaa Tahir
- *Red Queen* by Victoria Aveyard
- Honorable mentions that don't end in happily ever afters: *Romeo and Juliet, Wide Sargasso Sea*

29

RECLUSIVE HERO/HEROINE

DEFINITION

Ahh, the brooding, loner hero or heroine ... who can resist one of those? This trope is the story of the reclusive character who finally comes out of their grand isolation to find love, or the love interest who refuses to allow the recluse to remain locked away, literally or metaphorically, any longer. In either case, this is an archetypal tale of the breaching of the fortress of solitude.

This is usually the story of a wounded hero or heroine. Human beings are, by nature, social creatures. Therefore, when one chooses to remove himself or herself from contact with other people, something dramatic or traumatic has probably caused it. If a reclusive character has been antisocial their entire life, you as an author will have a very tall mountain to climb to convince readers/viewers that this truly antisocial person is capable of love, let alone interested in it.

A reclusive character can be simply a character type and not a full-blown trope. Often, the reclusive character type is portrayed as dark, dangerous, and brooding for the sake of being dark and brooding. Reclusiveness becomes a trope when that choice to withdraw from human contact interferes with finding love, and the story revolves around overcoming reclusiveness to find love.

At a minimum, this is a trope of lifestyle transformation. It is probably also a story of healing and personal transformation.

ADJACENT TROPES
--Shy Hero/Heroine
--Socially Awkward Hero/Heroine
--Lone Wolf Tamed
--Grumpy/Sunshine

WHY READERS/VIEWERS LOVE THIS TROPE
--dangerous love interests are incredibly sexy

--the fantasy of breaching the fortress to rescue the trapped prince or princess

--The fantasy of being rescued from being imprisoned or trapped in a terrible situation

--he or she changes for you

--he or she faces the dragon (their fears) for you.

--healing or fixing the broken person you love

--a person who lives outside society probably lives outside its rules of niceness ... which translates to dark, naughty, fantasy, taboo sex (or simply romance) and breaking all the rules with this recluse

OBLIGATORY SCENES
THE BEGINNING:
The love interest meets the recluse. Either it's an accidental meeting, or the love interest initiates first contact. The recluse is certainly NOT going to initiate contact with a stranger, particularly an attractive one of the gender to which he or she is attracted.

The recluse retreats to his or her fortress of solitude and firmly rejects the interest of the love interest...which poses an irresistible challenge to the love interest. And the games are on...

. . .

THE MIDDLE:

The middle of this story is a series of advances and retreats as the love interest tests and tries various methods and schemes to draw the recluse out of their physical or emotional shell. The recluse may emerge temporarily, but always retreats back into their fortress of solitude.

The source of the recluse's reclusiveness is revealed and explored by the recluse, or the love interest, or both of them. The love interest attempts to heal, or at least patch over the reclusive character's wound. This too, may have temporary success, but ultimately does not succeed.

BLACK MOMENT:

The love interest has thrown everything they have at drawing out the recluse. The recluse has done his or her level best to come out into the wider world, but it ultimately, and catastrophically fails.

The recluse rejects human society, retreats to his or her fortress of solitude, slams the gates and portcullis shut, and pulls up the draw-bridge. If the recluse had wagons inside his or her fortress, they would be circled up, too. This final, emphatic retreat also acts to reject the love interest, who is part of that human society the recluse has just, once and for all, shut out.

THE END:

Alone once more, the recluse finds that he or she is unable to bear the solitude anymore. Having now tasted the joy and comfort of companionship with the love interest, their solitary world becomes unbearable. Like it or not, they must come out of their shell and reach out for the love they've realized they crave more than they crave being alone.

The recluse emerges from his or her isolation and makes amends with the love interest, who welcomes him or her with open arms.

The recluse's wound may not be fully healed, but it certainly is on the way to getting better and is healed enough that the recluse is now capable of and desperate for love and companionship.

The love interest may have been allowed into the private world of the recluse, or the recluse may have emerged and joined the world the love interest comes from. Either way, the lovers find their happily ever after, together.

KEY SCENES

--first encounter between the recluse and love interest

--first physical contact between the lovers, which can be a touch, an embrace, a kiss, or more

--the big breakthrough moment for the recluse in leaving their fortress

--the retreat back to the fortress

--revelation of the recluse's wound

THINGS TO THINK ABOUT WHEN WRITING THIS TROPE

Why is the recluse a recluse? What has happened to make this person retreat from most or all human contact? Or does the recluse have a mental health or psychological condition such as agoraphobia which has no specific cause, but causes this person to end up isolated from others?

Why has the recluse responded to their trauma or condition by retreating from contact with other people?

Why hasn't the recluse sought therapy or help of some kind with their wound before now?

How do the recluse and the love interest meet? Is it an accident or intentional on one person's part (or both people's parts)?

What about the recluse does the love interest find fascinating and irresistible?

Likewise, what about the love interest does the recluse find interesting, intriguing, or attractive enough to capture and hold his or her interest?

What form does the recluse's fortress of solitude take? Is it physical or emotional?

It's likely that the recluse will carve out a private physical space for himself or herself to inhabit. Is it a cave, an office cubicle, a lab, a room, a house, a giant estate, or some other space?

If there is one, what secondary character provides the recluse with food and other supplies that allows him or her to remain apart from other people? How does that supporting character deliver supplies and take care of day-to-day needs of life for the recluse?

What's the relationship between the recluse and this secondary character? What does this support character think of the love interest? Does the support character help or hinder the love interest?

How does the recluse react when someone, who may or may not be the love interest, invades his or her personal lair?

Why does the love interest feel compelled to continue poking at the bear after initially getting snarled off by the recluse?

What about this pair's relationship keeps them coming back to each other in spite of the difficulties of being together?

What does the love interest think about the recluse's wound?

How will the recluse begin to overcome his or her trauma? Will he or she do it themselves or will the love interest drive the recluse's journey of facing the wound and addressing it?

What crisis drives the recluse back into his or her fortress to form the story's black moment? This needs to be a MAJOR setback...large enough to make a person in love abandon the person they've fallen for, larger enough to wreck one's life over.

How will the recluse face their wound? Is it a physical reckoning with a person, thing, or event? Is it an emotional reckoning with a past person, thing, or event?

How will the love interest help the recluse face their wound?

Does the love interest have a wound of his or her own that needs dealing with? (It's not uncommon for the love interest in this type of story to take their own trope-based journey.)

What does happily ever after look like for the recluse and their lover?

Will the love interest enter the world of the recluse and live there, or will the recluse ultimately join the world of the love interest?

TROPE TRAPS

Creating a recluse who's so reclusive, or so damaged, he or she would never plausibly rejoin the world of the living.

Not creating a wound, trauma, or mental health condition serious enough to justify a rational, intelligent person completely withdrawing from contact with other people.

Failing to give the love interest a logical and compelling enough reason for taking on the project of drawing out the recluse and forcing him or her to rejoin human society.

Creating a love interest who's merely pushing and annoying as they poke and provoke the recluse into coming out of their cave.

Creating a recluse who's mean. It's one thing to be wounded and striking out in one's pain, but it's another to just be cruel and thoughtless. (HINT: Make sure the reader knows why the recluse is being mean any time they strike out at those around him or her.)

Failing to paint a strong enough attraction/chemistry between the recluse and love interest to justify the recluse going to all the effort to overcome their isolation.

Not resolving the recluse's wound or failing to resolve it in a way that makes sense.

Waving a magic wand and fixing the recluse's entire wound just like that. A trauma so severe that it drove a human begin to cut themselves off form all other people is a VERY SERIOUS one. It's not likely to be fixed simply by the recluse and/or love interest deciding it's all fine, now. If it was that easy to fix, the recluse would've done it long ago.

Relying solely on the great sex or irresistible attraction between the recluse and love interest to magically fix the recluse's trauma.

Trauma is real and must be addressed with thoughtful strategies, therapy, and hard personal work. Many readers and viewers have experienced trauma and know this. They will howl if you short-change the seriousness of the mental health issue a true recluse probably is facing.

RECLUSIVE HERO/HEROINE IN ACTION
Movies:

- *The Batman*
- *Beauty and the Beast*
- *Drive*
- *Stranger Than Fiction*
- *Lars and the Real Girl*

Books:

- *Wuthering Heights* by Emily Bronte, the grandaddy of all recluse stories, although with a caveat that this love story does NOT end well
- *Flowers from the Storm* by Laura Kinsale
- *Archer's Voice* by Mia Sheridan
- *The Wall of Winnipeg and Me* by Mariana Zapata
- *Lover Awakened* by J.R. Ward
- *A Virgin River Christmas* by Robyn Carr
- *Dance With the Devil* by Sherrilyn Kenyon

30

SHY HERO/HEROINE

DEFINITION

Where the reclusive hero or heroine is so traumatized they physically withdraw from contact with other people, the shy hero or heroine merely is uncomfortable in the presence of other people, particularly those whom they don't know well. This discomfort typically leads to social awkwardness which makes forming relationships and finding love nigh impossible for the shy character.

Shy characters are capable of love. They may desperately desire love. They may be actively seeking love. They just can't overcome their shyness to find love. Until, of course, the love interest enters the romantic picture.

This is a trope of personal transformation, of overcoming shyness, coming out of one's emotional shell, learning to trust another person (or perhaps oneself), and opening up to the idea of love and to the love interest.

The shy hero or heroine may have always been shy, or some event or trauma in their life has left them shy about engaging with other people.

The line between a shy hero/heroine and a reclusive

hero/heroine may be purely a matter of degree of isolation. The shy hero/heroine probably interacts more and more directly with other people and the world at large than the recluse would, but they both have difficulty interacting with other people and don't like doing it. Whereas the recluse creates a full-blown fortress of solitude around himself or herself and rarely if ever leaves it, the shy person may merely retreat to a secret or private place when overwhelmed. While the recluse may never fully overcome their trauma, the shy person probably stands a chance of completely overcoming their shyness by the end of the story.

Often this is as much a story of establishing trust between two people as it is a story of overcoming shyness.

ADJACENT TROPES

--Socially Awkward Hero/Heroine
--Reclusive Hero/Heroine
--Grumpy/Sunshine

WHY READERS/VIEWERS LOVE THIS TROPE

--who doesn't love having the power to draw out a shy person?
--the shy person overcomes their shyness just for you
--taming the wild or fey creature (which the shy person represents)
--being allowed into the secret, private world of the shy person
--we love to be completely, unquestioningly trusted

OBLIGATORY SCENES
THE BEGINNING:

The shyness of the shy person is established, and the private or secret world they frequently or habitually retreat to is introduced.

The reason for the shy person being the way they are may be introduced right up front (or may unfold later in the story).

The love interest meets the shy person, and the shy person probably flees physically or emotionally. The love interest is intrigued and drawn to the shy person, and vice versa.

THE MIDDLE:

If it hasn't already been established in the beginning, the reason for the shy person's shyness is shown to the reader and to the love interest.

The love interest enters into a game of cat-and-mouse with the shy person, trying to lure or trick them out of their shyness and out of the place they retreat to. The shy person may or may not be a willing participant in being lured out of the secret sanctum. This part of the story involves a great deal of advance and retreat, one step forward and two steps back. The love interest may overtly try to instill confidence in the shy person in this phase of the story if the shy person lacks it.

The love interest may be invited into the secret, private place the shy person hides in. Their romance may unfold mostly in this place. And/or, the love interest may successfully draw the shy hero/heroine out into public where their romance can unfold.

A private "world" or emotional bubble may evolve around the shy character and love interest even when they are out in the real world among other people.

As attraction, and eventually love, develop between this pair, both are hopeful that the shy person's shyness can be overcome so a fulfilling, long-term relationship can be achieved.

BLACK MOMENT:

The shy person experiences a crisis that throws them all the way back to where the story started, or even further, into their shyness and mistrust of others. The shy person retreats to their private place, locks out the love interest, and flatly refuses to emerge again.

The relationship appears doomed, and the love interest has completely failed in their quest to draw out the shy person. All is lost.

THE END:

One or both characters manage to reach the shy person and convince him or her to give love and the love interest one last try. This final effort to overcome shyness succeeds, and the couple can finally be happy together. The shy person fully trusts the love interest, and the love interest fully trusts the shy person never to pull away again.

While the shy person may still maintain a secret or private retreat from the world at large, the love interest is always welcome there and has the key to the secret door.

KEY SCENES

--first visit by love interest to the secret or private world

--introduction of the love interest to trusted friends or family

--the reason why the shy person is shy revealed to love interest

--first romantic encounter

--the key to the secret sanctum is given to love interest, which is to say, permanent permission to visit is granted

THINGS TO THINK ABOUT WHEN WRITING THIS TROPE

Why is the shy hero/heroine shy?

Is the hero/heroine's shyness just the way they were born, or is it the result of some event or trauma? If so, what is that event or trauma?

How serious is the hero/heroine's shyness? Can her or she function normally in spite of it? Does it merely make them socially awkward? Is it socially crippling to him or her?

Who is the shy person actually comfortable with? Are there any family or friends with whom the shy person interacts with when they're outside of their private place?

What do the shy person's family and friends think of the love interest in the beginning, middle, and end of the story?

How is the hero/heroine's shyness manifested?

What form does the secret space or private retreat of the shy person take? Is it a supply closet at work? A room no one else is allowed to enter? A garden? An isolated home? Or is it not a physical space at all? Perhaps playing or listening to music? Escaping into creating art? Intense focus on a hobby? Reading? Running alone?

What triggers the shy person to need to escape into their private world?

How interested is the shy person at the beginning of the story in finding love?

How do the shy person and love interest meet? How does that meeting go? What are their first impressions of each other?

What attracts these two people to each other strongly enough that they're both willing to and interested in pursuing a relationship with each other despite the obstacles they will face?

What do the shy hero/heroine and love interest have in common?

Why is the love interest willing to stick around and do the hard work of drawing out the shy person or getting invited into the shy person's secret sanctum?

Does the love interest understand the shy person's shyness or is it completely new and strange to him or her?

How large of a concession is it for the shy character to let the love interest into their secret or private retreat?

What crisis provokes the shy person to run away from their love interest forcefully enough to end the relationship? Is it an external crisis or an internal one, or both?

How will the shy person overcome this crisis? Will he or she do it alone or with help—from friends and family, or from the love interest?

Will the shy person ultimately share his or her private space with the love interest, or will the private retreat be dismantled (or become public) by the end of the story?

TROPE TRAPS

Not justifying why the shy hero or heroine is as shy as they are.

No justifying why the love interest would spend all the time and hard work of getting to know the shy person and helping him or her come out of their shell.

Not creating a compelling or interesting private space or retreat for the shy person, or not creating a private enough space to actually insulate the shy person from the greater world.

Not creating an interesting or compatible enough love interest to justify the shy person doing the hard work necessary to make love possible.

Creating a love interest with an unappealing savior complex. As much as any one person my try to 'fix' another one, at the end of the day, we all are responsible for fixing ourselves...and audience members know this. As common a fantasy as it is to fix a broken hero or heroine, the reality is that people rarely change in any meaningful way. Which is to say, tread lightly with having the love interest swoop in and fix the shy hero or heroine.

Creating a shy hero or heroine who is just terribly awkward and anti-social as opposed to endearingly shy. While awkwardness and anti-social behaviors may be symptoms of shyness, in and of themselves, they can be off-putting to readers or viewers.

Creating a shy character who is thoughtless and hurtful to others. If your shy hero/heroine is going to behave this way, make sure the reader knows why they're behaving badly and doesn't end up hating your shy character.

Creating a love interest who seems masochistic for trying to have a relationship with such a damaged person.

Magically solving the shy character's shyness with great sex or being told "I love you."

Failing to paint a believable journey of growth toward more confidence for the shy person.

Transitioning the shy person to the life of the party too rapidly (or at all).

SHY HERO/HEROINE TROPE IN ACTION
Movies:

- *Rocky*
- *Sixteen Candles*
- *Amelie*
- *While You Were Sleeping*
- *Endless Love*
- *How to Fall in Love*
- *Superman*
- *The Perks of Being a Wallflower*
- *Lucas*

Books:

- *Easy* by Tammara Weber
- *The Madness of Lord Ian Mackensie* by Jennifer Ashley
- *Flat-Out Love* by Jessica Park
- *Unleash the Night* by Sherrilyn Kenyon
- *Rising Tides* by Nora Roberts
- *Rainwater* by Sandra Brown
- *Devil in Winter* by Lisa Kleypas

- *Breathe* by Kristen Ashley
- *Playing for Keeps* by R.L. Mathewson
- *Gabriel's Inferno* by Sylvain Reynard
- *Romancing Mr. Bridgerton* by Julia Quinn

31

SINGLE PARENT

DEFINITION

Simply put, this is a story about a single parent finding love and about a love interest falling in love with both a parent and their child.

Clearly, being a single parent could just as easily be a character type and not a full-blown trope if a cute little kid merely runs around in the background of the story being adorable. This could also be classed as an external trope where the existence of a child is an external or logistical problem to be overcome in falling in love and finding happily ever after. The single parent trope could even be classed as a hook trope if the child is an important or primary part of how the parent and love interest meet.

But, when the single parent and/or the love interest have to overcome the issues of one partner being a parent, a child being an integral part of the relationship, and the love interest stepping into the role of instant parent, then this can justifiably be classed as an internal trope.

In reality, when writing this trope, the 'parent-ness' of one character and the existence of a child may act as several tropes at once. Being a parent will most certainly be a defining aspect of the parental character. There is little on earth that changes the life of a person more profoundly than becoming a parent. This will also be an important aspect of the love interest's journey in this story type, for he or she, too, is going to be a parent by the end of the story. Indeed, this trope has the potential to be a story more about the love interest than the actual parent.

This is one of those tropes that may be misleadingly named. In many cases this trope could be more accurately called, Single Person Falls in Love with Single Parent and child, forming a new family. I've heard this trope alternately called, "And Baby Makes Three." The point is this is not just a love story between two people. Ultimately, it's a love story between three people—parent, love interest, and child.

In all cases, this is a story of personal transformation as the single parent opens his or her heart to love another adult and include him or her as a co-parent to their child. Or the personal transformation happens as the love interest opens their heart to become both lover and parent. Often both of these arcs are included in this type of story.

This is also a story of formation of a new family or of a replacement family. In all cases, it's a story of building deep trust. After all, sharing responsibility for the raising of one's child is one of the greatest bestowals of trust there is.

ADJACENT TROPES
--Widowed Hero/Heroine
--Insta-family
--Secret Baby
--Sacrifice

WHY READERS/VIEWERS LOVE THIS TROPE
--have you ever spent an hour chasing around a toddler? Who wouldn't want an adult partner with whom to share that monumental task?

--I'm still sexy and attractive even if I'm a parent

--having someone else love your perfect offspring as much as you do

--forming a new and better family than an absent, flawed, or broken one

--someone to share your burdens with you and make your life easier

--there is romance, good sex, and love after parenthood

--sleep. Sleep after having children...perhaps the most elusive and alluring fantasy of all

OBLIGATORY SCENES
THE BEGINNING:

The single parent and love interest meet. The child may or may not be present, and the existence of said child may or may not initially be revealed. Attraction sparks between these two...and then the subject of the child comes up.

The potential love interest sees something appealing enough in the single parent to stick around and get to know him or her better. Likewise, the single parent sees potential parent material in the potential love interest.

The child is introduced into the equation.

THE MIDDLE:

This section can be summed up as: parental shenanigans ensue.

The child and love interest meet. The parent's relationship with the love interest begins to develop, and the child, intentionally or otherwise, starts throwing monkey wrenches into it.

An ex or the missing parent of the child may show up and throw more monkey wrenches into the budding romance.

Concerned people around the couple may express approval or

disapproval and throw yet more monkey wrenches into this couple's relationship.

The single parent may test the love interest, throwing them into parental situations to see how well they handle the child and themselves.

The single parent may actually try to push away the love interest.

Meanwhile, the love interest is building a relationship with the child at the same time her or she is building a relationship with the parent, potentially complicating the entire dynamic of both relationships.

The love interest has to decide whether or not he or she is interested in and ready to become a caring parent to the child. This decision may be a foreign one to consider, may be difficult to make, and will carry a great deal of weight in all of their lives, therefore the decision cannot be made lightly.

BLACK MOMENT:

The relationship collapses. Potentially a crisis creates an impossible choice between parenting responsibility and personal feelings in the single parent. Perhaps the love interest has a crisis of belief in self to be a good parent. Perhaps the child declares his or her dislike of the idea of parent and love interest being together in a long-term relationship.

The different methods for breaking up this threesome are many and varied. But the end result is that the romance appears finished and unrecoverable. No happy family or happily ever after is going to emerge from this disaster.

THE END:

The disaster is solved. The love interest is ready to commit to being a partner, parent, and lover to the single parent. The single parent is ready to share responsibility for their child with the love interest. The child is also on board with parent and love interest both becoming his or her parents. They finally can be together as one happily ever after family.

KEY SCENES

--existence of child revealed

--first meeting between love interest and child

--first public appearance of single parent, love interest, and child in public together

--first romantic encounter between the adults

--child gives permission for the three of them to become a family

THINGS TO THINK ABOUT WHEN WRITING THIS TROPE

How did the single parent become a single parent?

How old is the child?

What type of care does the child require, and how much time does all of that take? Which is to say, how much time does the single parent have for dating and when does that time happen?

Does the single parent have any friends or family to help them or is he/she totally on hie or her own? This will inform how much free time the single parent has for dating and what form that dating can take.

Does the love interest have any experience with children?

What is the love interest's opinion of children in general when the story begins? Does that opinion change over the course of the story? If so, how?

What does the child think of the love interest when they meet?

What do the love interest and child have in common? What do they do when they spend time together? How do they feel about hanging out together?

What is the single parent looking for in a parent to their child?

How does the love interest feel about an instant family in the beginning, middle, and end of the story?

Will the love interest end up adopting the child or not?

Where is the absent parent of the child? Does the absent parent have part in the child's or single parent's life? If so, what does that look like? If not, why not?

Is the love interest ever going to meet the absent parent? How does that go?

What crisis will collapse this budding family?

How will the single parent and love interest overcome the disaster that has torn them apart?

When do the love interest and child fall in love? When do they declare their love? This may be a separate event from the single parent and love interest declaring their feelings.

What does the new family look like when it's finally formed?

TROPE TRAPS

A single parent who magically has all the time in the world to primp, go out on dates, and act single

A love interest who has never been around children magically being completely prepared to handle all parental situations and getting parenting right every single time.

A perfect child.

A perfectly horrible child.

An evil, irresponsible ex who is so cliché as to seem cartoonish. Mind you, it's perfectly fine to create a terrible ex, but try to make him or her at least a little believable.

A medical emergency with the child that throws the single parent and love interest into crisis...and as soon as it's resolved, they all end up together happily ever after. Which is to say, a contrived crisis to tear the single parent and love interest apart.

No serious discussion of what being a parent actually entails.

No serious thought by the single parent about the qualifications of the love interest to be a decent parent.

Failing to establish and grow an actual relationship between the child and the love interest.

Painting children who are massively wiser and wittier than their age would plausibly allow them to be...even if they're the most precocious child on the planet. Five-year-olds rarely pop out with pithy and complex relationship advice. I'm just saying.

SINGLE PARENT TROPE IN ACTION
Movies:

- *The Parent Trap*
- *One Fine Day*
- *Jerry Maguire*
- *Maid in Manhattan*
- *The Sound of Music*
- *Kindergarten Cop*
- *Hope Floats*
- *Blended*
- *Chocolat*
- *Raising Helen*
- *The Back-up Plan*
- *Three Men and a Baby*

Books:

- *Ignite* by Melanie Harlow
- Juniper Hill by Devney Perry
- *Wait For It* by Mariana Zapata
- *Things We Never Got Over* by Lucy Score

- *Happily Letter After* by Vi Keeland
- *One Percent of You* by Michelle Gross
- *To Hate Adam Connor* by Ella Maise
- *Mr. Masters* by T.L. Swan
- *The Soulmate Equation* by Christina Lauren
- *Sweet Temptation* by Cora Reilly
- Life's Too Short by Abby Jimenez
- *Scandalous* by L.J. Shen
- *The Air He Breathes* by Brittainy C. Cherry
- *The Bride Test* by Helen Hoang
- *It Starts With Us* by Colleen Hoover

32

SOCIALLY AWKWARD
HERO/HEROINE

DEFINITION

This is the story of a socially awkward character struggling and finally managing to fall in love. On the spectrum of reclusive hero/heroine, shy hero/heroine, and socially awkward hero/heroine, this is the must functional character of the three. The socially awkward hero/heroine actually functions in society and is able for the most part being around other people...he or she just isn't very good at it.

Traditionally, this character functions amazingly well in a crisis or is incredibly skilled at what they do. They just don't seem to have any idea how to behave in a smooth, sophisticated, socially adept way around other people, particularly of the gender they're attracted to. This excellence at some other endeavor is a way of making it clear that this person is fully capable of functioning intelligently or excellently...they just have a problem with social situations.

Something to think about when writing this trope is that there may be an underlaying cause of this her or heroine's social awkwardness that will require sensitivity in how you write it. Some people on the neurodivergent spectrum may exhibit social awkwardness as part of their particular condition. Even if it is not your intent to write a neurodivergent character be cognizant of whether or not your character comes across as possibly having an underlying neurological cause for his or her behavior.

ADJACENT TROPES
--Burdened by Beauty/Talent
--Nerd/Geek/Genius
--Clumsy/Bumbling/Thoughtless Hero/Heroine
--Shy Hero/Heroine
--Opposites Attract

Why Readers/VIEWERS Love This Trope
--don't we all feel socially awkward at one time or another?

--feeling lovable even though we, too, have our own socially awkward moments

--we've all been embarrassed by saying the wrong thing at the wrong time to the wrong person. It's good to know this hero/heroine lives to see another day after doing the same thing

--knowing that it's okay to make a fool of yourself from time to time

--sometimes embarrassing yourself is endearing to others

OBLIGATORY SCENES
THE BEGINNING:
The socially awkward hero/heroine and their future love interest meet. The socially awkward character typically makes a fool of himself or herself and typically is embarrassed by having done so. Some of the funniest, most cringe-worthy meet-cutes in all of fiction come from the antics these socially awkward characters get up to.

The love interest finds something about the socially awkward character attractive, although that awkward soul may have a hard time fathoming what it could be. The socially awkward character feels deeply uncomfortable with the potential love interest.

THE MIDDLE:

Shenanigans definitely ensue. This is often a comic trope and we're treated to various laughably painfully scenes as the socially awkward main character bumbles through try after try and getting it right in a social setting...and failing every time, more spectacularly than the last.

In the non-comedy setting, the socially awkward character may try, with the help of the love interest to figure out how to navigate various social situations.

As a romance begins to develop between these two characters, each advance of the relationship to the next level is a new opportunity for the socially awkward character not to know how to function in that moment. The developing romance may go comically badly, or tragically wrong.

A great deal of the tone of this story will be set by how the love interest reacts to the socially awkward character's gaffs. If the love interest finds it funny, charming, or sweet, the tone of the story is likely to be similarly funny, charming, or sweet. But, if the love interest reacts with embarrassment, awkwardness or pity for the socially awkward character, the tone of the story will be considerably darker and potentially tragic.

BLACK MOMENT:

The socially awkward character says or does something that completely ruins any chance for the relationship to continue. Perhaps the love interest has been horribly humiliated (often in public), or perhaps the socially awkward character himself or herself has been utterly humiliated. Perhaps the socially awkward character has committed an unforgivable social faux pas. Or perhaps, other people have reacted to the socially awkward character's mistake in a way that makes it impossible for the love interest to remain with him or her. Regardless of what exactly went wrong, the relationship is ruined by a socially awkward mistake, most of the time made by the main character, and seems beyond repair.

THE END:

The situation that created the black moment is rectified. Perhaps there's an apology made and forgiveness given. Or perhaps the character(s) who harshly judged the socially awkward character reverse their opinion after realizing there was no malicious intent behind the socially awkward faux pas. Fixing the situation may require the love interest to forgive the socially awkward character for humiliating them.

The mistake that broke up the lovers is forgiven or fixed, and the socially awkward hero/heroine and their love interest can finally be together.

Sometimes, the socially awkward character has become much less awkward over the course of the story and the completion of that journey is also part of the story's happy ending. We see this character functioning reasonably well in a social situation, now.

Conversely, the socially awkward character may remain awkward, but at least by the end of the story they and their love interest are much less self-conscious about it, and it ceases to be an obstacle to happiness for them.

KEY SCENES

--the meet-cute...or more accurately, meet-embarrassing

--the first time the love interest is embarrassed by the socially awkward hero/heroine

--the first romantic scene, which can either go incredibly well or incredibly awkwardly

--demonstration of the extreme competence of the socially awkward hero/heroine at something

--the moment the socially awkward hero/heroine is humiliated by making an epic, and serious, public gaff in front of the love interest

--the moment of forgiveness by the love interest for the big mistake

THINGS TO THINK ABOUT WHEN WRITING THIS TROPE

What form does the hero or heroine's social awkwardness take? Choosing to make this character shy is such a common choice that over time, the Shy Hero/Heroine has really become a trope in its own right. Social awkwardness can take many forms—inability to say the right thing or find the right words, inability to criticize others, inability to speak coherently in large crowds or in front of others, paralyzing self-consciousness, or self-doubt, for example.

Is there something your socially awkward hero or heroine is outstanding at? He or she doesn't have to have some special skill or gift, of course, Ask yourself if your character needs or would benefit from some contrasting ability that contrasts with his or her social awkwardness.

How do the socially awkward hero/heroine and the future love interest meet? How does the love interest treat the socially awkward character in that encounter?

What is the love interest's first impression of the socially awkward hero or heroine?

What is the socially awkward person's first impression of the potential love interest?

How pervasive and crippling is the main character's social awkwardness? Does it show itself around friends and family? Does it pop up when in private with the love interest or not?

Is the main character's social awkwardness based merely in not knowing the rules and norms of the social circle he or she is moving in, or is it a deeper problem than that? If it's the former, do you have enough plot and character development to sustain the main arc of your story?

Will the love interest try to help coach the socially awkward character through any social situations? What situations? How does it go?

Is your story primarily comic or serious, or some of each? What sorts of social situations fit the tone of your story to show the main character's social awkwardness?

Is the socially awkward character looking for love? Does he or she believe he or she can reasonably find love, or do they see it as a hopeless search?

Does the plot of your story set up abundant social situations that the awkward hero or heroine must function in? Which is to say, do you have the right type of plot for this trope?

How un-awkward and socially adept will the main character be by the end of the story? How will he or she transition from beginning awkwardness to this end point?

Is there an underlying emotional issue or trauma that has made this character socially awkward? (this isn't a requirement, just a possible choice.)

What are some past disastrous social situations gone awry in the main character's life that have left emotional scars, emotional baggage, self-consciousness, or shame? How do those scars and wounds manifest themselves in your story?

Because this trope tends to describe primarily the journey of one person, will you use another trope to flesh out the emotional journey of the love interest? If so, what is it? Are these tropes both comic, both serious, or split into one comic arc and one serious arc?

What is the emotional arc of the love interest with regard to this specific trope through your story? Does he or she start out dismissive or scornful of the main character and learn to love him or her? Does the love interest find the main character adorable but have trouble expressing their romantic interest to the awkward character? Does the love interest feel sorry for the socially awkward character and have to learn to respect that character's agency?

Does the socially awkward character mostly embarrass himself or herself, or does this person manage to humiliate himself or herself in the story? We all get embarrassed from time to time, but full out humiliation is devastating, with potential to cause much more emotional damage. (HINT: in a background on ongoing embarrassments, humiliation is ideal for the black moment.)

How embarrassed and/or humiliated is the love interest at various socially awkward moments in the story? Does this bother him or her? If not, why not? If so, how much, and what does he or she do about it?

What is the external plot—the stuff that's happening in the book —that moves the story forward seamlessly from social interaction to social interaction?

How socially awkward is the love interest?

Does the love interest ever fake social awkwardness for the benefit of the socially awkward main character?

How does the socially awkward character turn out in the end? Is he or she "fixed"? Does he or she continue to make gaffs, but with a sense of humor about it, now? Does the love interest plan to coach the awkward character through social encounters for the rest of their lives?

TROPE TRAPS

Failing to build a believable plot that pulls readers or viewers forward through the story. A book based around a character fumbling in social situations is prone to end up being a string of embarrassment scenes and lose a sense of flow and forward movement, which can kill your pacing.

Lack of sufficient character growth in the awkward character's story arc. If the love interest can simply sit down and teach the awkward character the rules of the social circle, and voila everything is fixed, this might make for a decent secondary trope arc, but there's probably not enough conflict and required growth to support the main thread of a story.

Humiliating the socially awkward character so badly they flee the social circle or environment and never plausibly return.

Creating a character so embarrassing to be around that no reasonable person would fall in love with him or her.

Not creating enough of a romantic spark for the awkward character to be willing to do the hard work of overcoming their affliction to find love.

Setting up a long-term dynamic where the socially awkward character will be overly dependent on the love interest to always bail him or her out of social mistakes. Which is to say, setting up the love interest as too much of a parental figure.

Making readers/viewers feel mainly sorry for the awkward character and never perceiving him or her as a potential romantic lead.

Making the socially awkward character terrible at everything they do and giving them no redeeming qualities or proficiencies at anything.

Setting up the love interest to pity the awkward character and not see them as romantically attractive.

Giving the love interest a savior complex.

Failing to show what the love interest will get out of this relationship.

SOCIALLY AWWARD HERO/HEROINE TROPE IN ACTION
Movies:

- *Scott Pilgrim vs. the World*
- *Punch Drunk Love*
- *American Pie*
- *My Big Fat Greek Wedding*

- *Muriel's Wedding*
- *The Pink Panther*

Books:

- *Neanderthal Seeks Human* by Penny Reid
- *Were-Geeks Save Wisconsin* by Kathy Lyons
- *The Hooker and the Hermit* by L.H. Cosway
- *The Rosie Project* by Graeme Simsion
- *The Flatshare* by Beth O'Leary
- *Nerd in Shining Armor* by Vicki Lewis Thompson

33

UGLY DUCKLING

DEFINITION

This is the story of a character who goes from ugly, literally or metaphorically, to beautiful, and by the end of that journey finds true love. In the original fable by this name, a duck hatches a clutch of eggs. All the ducklings are yellow, adorable balls of fluff except for one that is gray, gangly, awkward, and bigger than the others. Everyone declares him to be the ugly duckling and his feelings are hurt as they ostracize him. But the next year when all the ducks, now grown up, return to the pond, the ugly duckling has grown into a swan, more beautiful by far than all of his brothers and sisters. They all love him, now.

It's worth noting that this is not a makeover story. The difference between the ugly duckling and makeover tropes is how long it takes for the main character to transform. The makeover happens quite quickly, whereas the ugly duckling changes gradually over a relatively long period of time into their swan-self.

This is a story of (typically natural) transformation, over a long period of time. In most ugly duckling stories, the main characters have known each other in the past, when one of them deemed the other "ugly".

A long time has passed, and now circumstances have thrown them into each other's paths once more. The love interest, along with the other ducks in the pond, is stunned to see how different the hero/heroine is from how they remembered the ugly duckling. Love blossoms, and happily ever after is not far behind.

Like the makeover trope, this one comes with a warning label: be cautious and sensitive about what you label to be 'ugly' in your duckling character. Also, the notion of being lovable now that one has become beautiful is problematic. The swan was always lovable, even as an awkward, clumsy, funny-shaped cygnet, and the bias of the love interest not to have seen that earlier is not especially heroic.

There are any number of ways to plot around this problem:

--Perhaps the duckling wasn't the least bit interested in what the love interest thought back then.

--The duckling character wasn't ugly, rather they were merely clumsy, disproportionately shaped, or had, say, Hermione Grainger's head of wild hair.

-- It's entirely possible to give a character an attribute that isn't disfiguring in scale, like crooked teeth, and will be easy enough to fix later.

-- Or a character can simply transform from unremarkable (but not completely unfortunate looking, to quote Elle Woods).

In the book list for this trope, I've chosen several fun variations on this trope: a character who don't remember her transformation, a heroine who transforms from swan to duckling and has to find a new definition of beauty, and a character whose transformation makes someone want to kill her.

ADJACENT TROPES
--Makeover
--Spinster/Bluestocking/On the Shelf
--Plain Jane/John
--Girl/Boy Next Door

--Right Under Your Nose

WHY READERS/VIEWERS LOVE THIS TROPE

--who doesn't want to turn into a beautiful swan? (especially since we all tend to see ourselves as ugly ducklings in one way or another)

--the revenge is sweet

--getting a do-over on the past

--tossing off one's old life and stepping into a new and glamorous one

--all the hard work is worth it

--now who's embarrassed?

OBLIGATORY SCENES
THE BEGINNING:

This is the rare trope that may actually come with a prologue (in the form of an actual, formal prologue or perhaps just a flashback scene) where the ugly duckling and love interest cross paths, well in the past. In this scene, the ugly duckling is portrayed as, well, ugly, in the eyes of the future love interest. The ugly duckling reacted to that in the past however you'd like them to, based on the conflict you're setting up for the story.

In lieu of a full-blown prologue, the love interest may see old pictures of the ugly duckling or have heard about how they were in the past. Or we may merely see the love interest remembering the ugliness of the duckling character prior to their current-day meeting.

In the time that passes between the past and present moment, the ugly duckling has transformed into a swan. This can have happened by growing up, getting access to cosmetic or medical care, a change in lifestyle over time, or any number of other means of gradual transformation as one grew up or matured.

The ugly duckling and love interest meet. The love interest is shocked and amazed by the ugly duckling's transformation. This may or may not please our swan, who may or may not enjoy the attention, may or may not enjoy sweet revenge, or who may be wholly annoyed by the love interest's reaction to the swan version of them.

THE MIDDLE:

In most cases, the love interest settles in for some good old-fashioned groveling and making up. The swan typically is the one who holds out on falling head over heels in love. The swan is usually looking for the love interest to prove he or she is not shallow, superficial, judgmental, and otherwise a jerk. Meanwhile, the love interest spends much of the middle of the story wrapping his or her head around the change in the duckling-to-swan.

The swan may put the love interest through a series of tests to discover the love interest's true values.

The love interest often expresses not caring about the transformation...now that it is complete. This usually rings hollow to the swan and is a source of conflict for the lovers.

BLACK MOMENT:

The duckling-turned-swan doesn't believe the love interest's sincerity when the lover declares his or her love, and the relationship collapses in disaster. The swan simply can't bring themselves to trust the steadfastness of the lover's feelings based on how they've change from the ugly duckling days to now. All is lost.

THE END:

The love interest makes a grand declaration or demonstration of their true love for the swan that the duckling-turned-swan finally accepts and believes. They have overcome the duckling's trust issues and finally can be together forever in true love.

If the ugly duckling was at all uncomfortable with his or her own transformation or the love interest's reaction to the change, that is all resolved by the end. The swan has grown into his or her skin fully and is at ease in their own skin, now.

KEY SCENES
--the moment of meeting the swan
--the moment of recalling the ugliness of the duckling
--the love interest takes the swan out in public
--confrontation of the love interest by the swan over their change of heart
--moment of forgiveness by the swan of the love interest

THINGS TO THINK ABOUT WHEN WRITING THIS TROPE
In what way has the duckling transformed into a swan?

Did the ugly duckling merely grow into their body, grow into good looks, or have some kind of work done like braces or cutting/growing out hair and getting good hair care products?

How dramatic is the transformation from duckling to swan?

Has the transformation changed the duckling-to-swan's life in any other major way?

Does the duckling-turned-swan have any lingering emotional baggage, scars, or wounds from his or her duckling days?

Did the love interest see any hint of the swan to come way back in the old days when he or she knew the ugly duckling?

How did the love interest treat the duckling back in the old days? How did the duckling feel about that?

How strongly does the love interest react to meeting the swan? Does her or she show that reaction to the now swan?

How distrustful is the swan of the love interest's reaction to meeting him or her?

What about the love interest attracts the swan to the current-day love interest? Be sure to differentiate this attractive quality or qualities from any old attraction the duckling might have had to the past love interest.

Is the love interest someone the duckling had a crush on in the past? Is the love interest someone the duckling believed to be out of reach as a friend or boyfriend or girlfriend in the past? What made the past love interest seem unattainable to the ugly duckling? Did the duckling misjudge the past love interest or see him or her correctly back then?

What does the love interest do to prove to the swan that his or her feelings now are sincere?

How does the swan test the truthfulness and values of the love interest before committing to a relationship with him or her?

What does the love interest do to spectacularly mess up the relationship with the swan in what becomes the black moment of this trope?

How does the love interest apologize for their huge mistake in a way that the swan is willing to consider accepting the apology?

How does the love interest demonstrate that he or she fully embraces and loves the duckling that still resides inside the swan, and that the duckling was lovable all along?

What attracts the duckling and/or swan to the love interest?

TROPE TRAPS

Failing to address the shift of the duckling from the one who would've been reaching up in partners to being the swan whom the love interest is now reaching up to date.

Forgetting to show readers or viewers what the love interest thought of the duckling in his or her "ugly" form.

Offending your audience with how the ugliness of the duckling is portrayed.

Creating a love interest who was such a jerk in the past that readers, viewers, and the swan cannot plausibly forgive him or her now, nor does the jerk deserve to end up with the swan.

Painting the love interest as so superficial and shallow that only the exterior appearance of the duckling-turned-swan matters or attracts him or her to the swan.

Failing to give the duckling-turned-swan a believable journey of transformation.

Failing to address the emotional journey of the duckling as he or she becomes a swan along with his or her physical transformation.

Failing to show the love interest learning that the exterior appearance of the swan is really less important than the inner beauty the duckling and swan have always had.

Not giving the love interest a growth arc in the intervening time between first knowing each other and now. The duckling isn't the only one who has changed and grown.

UGLY DUCKLING TROPE IN ACTION
Movies:

- *She's All That*
- *The Girl Most Likely To...*
- *Ugly Betty* (TV show)
- *The Enchanted Cottage*
- *The Shape of Things*
- *My Life in Ruins*
- *Never Been Kissed*
- *My Fair Lady*

Books:

- *The Ugly Duchess* by Eloisa James

- *Bet Me* by Jennifer Crusie
- Devil In Winter by Lisa Kleypas
- *Beautiful* by Danielle Steele
- Something Wonderful by Judith McNaught
- *Where I Belong* by J. Daniels
- The Do-Over by M.K. Schiller
- *Open Season* by Linda Howard
- *Remember Me?* by Sophie Kinsella

34

VIRGIN HERO/HEROINE

DEFINITION

The hero or heroine is never made love, and this poses an impediment to the relationship that must be overcome. Obviously, in point of physical fact, this is a fairly easy impediment to overcome. Therefore, to turn it into an entire trope, there must be a compelling reason the virgin character hasn't made love before now and why it's a problem to consummate an emotional relationship in a physical way.

For some reason, the virgin hero or heroine fears sex or the consequences of sex, or perhaps they've made a vow of celibacy they only feel free to break when certain conditions are met. Personal beliefs—religious, cultural, or familial—could make making love before marriage taboo for this character. Or perhaps this character fears a pregnancy for some reason.

A character could have been assaulted in the past. While their body may have been through the physical act, they may never have made love to a person whom they have feelings for. For the purposes of this trope, this character is most certainly a virgin in the emotional and psychological sense of the word.

This is a trope that could easily rely on external reasons for the hero or heroine being a virgin, society or family forbidding sex before a permanent and approved relationship is established, for example.

But in the case of the internal trope version, the hero or heroine personally has some compelling reason for not having made love before now. It is that reason which must be overcome for this couple to find their happily ever after.

In this type of story, it's not uncommon for there to be a combination of external and internal reasons for the virgin character never having made love before.

ADJACENT TROPES
--Celibate Hero/Heroine
--Fear of Intimacy
--Goody Two Shoes
--First Love
--Spinster/Bluestocking/On the Shelf

WHY READERS/VIEWERS LOVE THIS TROPE
--imagining a new and different do-over one one's first sexual experience
--the fantasy of introducing someone hot to sex
--being in charge of the sex
--shaping a lover into the kind of lover you crave
--emotional innocence recaptured

OBLIGATORY SCENES
THE BEGINNING:
The hero and heroine meet and are attracted to each other. The relationship quickly moves toward sex, or the topic comes up in conversation. Pretty straightforward, huh? But then one of them

introduces a complication. They've never made love, and they're not ready to do so now, for some reason.

The love interest is attracted enough to stick around and likes the virgin hero/heroine for more than just sex. (Yay! We love this love interest!)

THE MIDDLE:

The romance progresses and the feelings between the hero and heroine deepen to the point that making love is becoming a natural expression of their feelings and commitment.

The problem or multiple problems preventing the virgin character from jumping in the sack with the person they obviously care deeply about become obvious and get in the way of the relationship moving forward.

The decision by the virgin hero or heroine to remain virgin is challenged...typically with ever increasing degrees of temptation. The love interest's frustration typically mounts, as well.

The virgin alone or the couple together may start trying to address the problem getting in the way of their making love. If you've chosen a problem big enough to sustain the plot of the book, simple conversation and open communication between these two characters is not sufficient to resolve the problem.

In fact, the problem may get significantly worse as the story proceeds. Perhaps others around the couple are becoming aware of the relationship and forbidding it. Or perhaps old, traumatic memories are surfacing that impede the virgin hero or heroine from making love.

BLACK MOMENT:

The hero and heroine may get all the way to the point of consummating the relationship, but the virgin hero or heroine balks one last time. The love interest gives up on this character ever overcoming their problem(s) with sex to actually be able to make love.

OR

The virgin hero/heroine is on the verge of making love with the love interest when a crisis intervenes to stop them. This crisis is so serious that it not only stops the sex but tears apart the hero and heroine permanently.

While on its surface this might appear to be an external crisis, making this an external trope, the virgin hero/heroine does not solve, ignore, or push through the crisis to finally show their love in a physical way, and this makes the external problem an internal crisis.

THE END:

Whatever hang-up, taboo, rule, norm, or fear is stopping the virgin hero or heroine from making love with the person they've already given their heart to is finally resolved. Or at least, it's resolved enough that this person is now able and willing to make love with the person they love.

They way is clear for these two frustrated lovers to finally consummate their relationship physically.

Now that the list pieces of their relationship have finally fallen into place and the obstacles to love—emotional, psychological, and/or physical—have been removed, this couple can finally have their happily ever after. And sex. Lots of sex.

KEY SCENES

--confession that he or she is a virgin

--duh...the big moment of first sex

--revelation of the real reason why this character is unable or unwilling to make love

--the love interest giving permission to the virgin not to make love until he or she is ready

THINGS TO THINK ABOUT WHEN WRITING THIS TROPE

Why is the hero/heroine a virgin?

Is there some trauma in the hero or heroine's past associated with sex that may or may not be part of their calculus not to have sex?

Under what circumstances will this character gain permission from self or from others to make love with someone?

Why is this love interest the ONE?

How does the love interest feel about the virgin hero/heroine? What attracts the love interest to this person? Is the virgin hero or heroine/s virginity part of the attraction? (Tread lightly with how you answer this one, kids.)

How does the virgin character feel about their virginity? Is it something they cherish? Resent? Feel embarrassed by? Feel proud of? Want to get rid of? Fear getting rid of?

What makes the virgin's emotions complicated around the idea of making love?

Take the primary emotion(s) you've assigned to your virgin character with regard to their virginal state. How can you have this character experience the opposite emotion at some point in the story?

What changes that allow the virgin hero/heroine to make love with the person they love?

When in the story will the (first) making love scene, that is the losing of virginity scene, take place? What needs to come after this scene in the story, if anything, or is this where your story ends?

TROPE TRAPS

The timing of the first love scene. It's darned hard to raise the stakes any more in your story after these two beleaguered, long-suffering characters *finally* get to make love.

If the love scene is not the final scene in your book, failing to lift the action and emotional stakes enough to hold the interest of readers or viewers after they finally make it to and through this moment.

Creating a love interest who is not patient enough to plausibly be willing to wait for the virgin character to work through whatever they need to in order to be ready to make love.

Creating characters solely fixated on the sex portion of their relationship.

Not developing the other aspects of love between these two characters—trust, friendship, shared values and interests, commitment, etc.

Not justifying why the virgin character has remained virgin until now.

Painting a character, who was previously not interested in making love or okay with the reasons stopping him or her from making love, suddenly deciding that he or she has to do the deed as soon as humanly possible.

The virgin character putting so much pressure on the love interest being the ONE that any reasonable love interest would run screaming.

Failing to deliver a love scene worthy of the wait you've put both the characters and audience through.

VIRGIN HERO/HEROINE TROPE IN ACTION
Movies:

- *The 40-Year-Old Virgin*
- *Jane the Virgin*
- *The First Time*
- *Cruel Intentions*
- *Porky's*

- *The To Do List*
- *The Rules of Attraction*

Books:

- Outlander by Diana Gabaldon
- *Twilight* by Stefanie Meyer
- *Kiss an Angel* by Susan Elizabeth Phillips
- *Bound by Honor* by Cora Reilly
- A Hunger Like No Other by Kresley Cole
- *Beautiful Disaster* by Jamie McGuire
- *Fallen Too Far* by Abby Glines
- *Playing for Keeps* by R.L. Mathewson
- *Bully* by Penelope Douglas
- *Losing It* by Cora Carmack
- *The Mistake* by Elle Kennedy
- *In Flight* by R.K Lilley
- *Wait for You* by Jennifer L. Armentrout
- *Rule* by Jay Crownover
- *Hot Head* by Damon Suede
- *Pestilence* by Laura Thalassa
- *Caressed by Ice* by Nalini Singh
- *The Bride Test* by Helen Hoang

35

WIDOWED HERO/HEROINE

DEFINITION

This is the story of a character who has already been married once before, whose spouse has died, and who finds love again. The circumstances under which the widow or widower was married and under which their previous spouse died will determine much of the tone of this story.

Was the first marriage a love match or arranged for business reasons? Forced or voluntary? Was the death of the spouse anticipated or a surprise? Slow or abrupt? A recent loss or a distant one? Each of these choices will affect the type of love story that works for this main character and his or her love interest going forward.

Typically, this trope deals with the first serious relationship the widow/widower has entered into since losing their former spouse. Issues of getting back in the saddle and learning how to date after all this time, of guilt toward the memory of the deceased spouse, judgment by family and friends, and feeling disloyal to the former spouse are common in this type of story.

. . .

To write this trope requires you to plot not one but two love stories. One has concluded, and the second is just beginning, but the first will affect the second a great deal.

At its core, this is a story of healing. The widow or widower has suffered one of the most painful losses a human being can go through. The love interest typically does a great deal of heavy lifting in this trope to bring a sense of renewed hope, renewed belief in love, and renewed joy to the bereaved widow or widower.

Often this is a trope of finding belief that has been lost. It may be a belief in love or even a belief in life. The widow or widower may have lost faith in a deity, in fate, in luck, or in fairness. The bereaved character may not believe true love is possible a second time around.

The love interest may have to endure comparisons to the first spouse that challenge their commitment to the widow/widower and to the relationship.

Of all the obstacles to love that two people have to overcome, this trope may be one of the most challenging, certainly on an emotional level.

ADJACENT TROPES
--Single Parent
--Best Friend's Widow/Widower
--Fresh Start
--Rebound Romance
--Survivor Guilt

WHY READERS/VIEWERS LOVE THIS TROPE
--second chance at love, and at life
--light in a great darkness
--hope never dies
--these stories are often great tearjerkers and who doesn't love a good, sloppy cry?

--he or she will take a chance on love again for me

--healing the broken soul and broken heart

OBLIGATORY SCENES
THE BEGINNING:

The widow/widower and future love interest meet. The tone of this meeting will set the tone for the book, be it cute and perky or dark and tragic. Attraction may spark in the widow/widower but definitely sparks in the love interest.

The status of the main character as a widow/widower is revealed.

The love interest is mostly likely the one to more the relationship forward initially, depending on how wounded the widow/widower still is. The widow/widower may resist entering into any kind of relationship.

THE MIDDLE:

The relationship advances and retreats. In this part of the story, the love story typically drives the advances in the relationship, and the widow/widower typically drives the retreats. It's a dance of one step forward, two steps back.

The history of the previous marriage comes out. Initially, the widow/widower may portray it as having been perfect. But as the story unfolds, the truth is more likely to emerge. The widow/widower measures the love interest against the former spouse, and this may be a source of conflict between them.

The widow/widower's heart beings to wake once more. Feelings of remorse and guilt may accompany this return to the dating world. The love interest must be extremely sensitive and responsive to the widow/widower's potentially mercurial mood changes during the getting to know you and falling for you phases of the relationship.

Friends and family, maybe well-meaning or malicious, of the deceased spouse and/or family and friends of the widow/widower may interfere with the relationship or may try to aid and abet it. Typically, their interference is not appreciated by either the widow/widower or the love interest. This can be a source of conflict, humor, or both.

BLACK MOMENT:

The widow or widower goes into crisis. Whatever force has been making the hesitate to jump into a new relationship with the love interest comes to a head. He or she cannot go through with a new relationship and backs out of it.

The love interest runs out of patience for the widow/widower, and the pair split. They're just not able to overcome the ghost of the previous marriage in their own relationship. All is lost, and the widow/widower is plunged into a new round of grief from which they think they'll never emerge.

THE END:

Having broken up, both the widow/widower and the love interest are so miserable that they cannot bear being apart. As much difficulty and challenge as there was to overcome while together, that's better than this pain, now.

The pair come back together to work out their problems. Lessons have been learned, perhaps compromises made, and they finally reconcile. Healing happens. The widow/widower has miraculously found love a second time around, and the love interest has found love and helped this wounded soul heal.

KEY SCENES

--revelation that the main character is a widow/widower
--revelation of the details of the former spouse's death

--the first romantic scene (first kiss, first date, or first sex after losing the spouse)

--the moment when the widow/widower completely falls apart

--the first time the love interest meets the family and friends who knew the former spouse

THINGS TO THINK ABOUT WHEN WRITING THIS TROPE

How much did the widow/widower love or hate their former spouse? What kind of a marriage was it?

How long has it been since the former spouse died? How did the former spouse die?

How did the widow/widower deal with the death of the former spouse?

Are there children from the previous marriage? If not, why not?

Is this the first time the widow/widower has dated or entered into a relationship after losing their former spouse? If not, how many relationships since the death have there been? Have they been casual? Disastrous one-time dates?

What about the love interest is compelling enough to the widow/widower to consider dating again with this particular person?

How does the love interest feel about being compared to the former spouse?

How are the former spouse and the new love interest different? How are they the same? How does the widow/widower feel about these traits?

What do the family and friends of the deceased spouse think about the widow/widower dating again?

What do the widow/widower's friends and family think of him or her dating again? Do these people interfere or not? Are they helpful? Well-meaning? Bumbling? In the way?

What are the primary emotions the widow/widower feels toward the love interest? What are the opposites of these feelings, and can the widow/widower also experience one or more of these negative feelings along the way?

How does the widow/widower resolve the fact that they're dating again? Do they feel as if they're betraying the memory of the dead spouse?

Did the former spouse exhort them to see other people and love again?

Does the widow/widower hold up their deceased spouse as a saintly figure to whom all others (and certainly the love interest) are compared? If not, why not?

What is it that makes the widow/widower pull back at the last moment before going through with this new relationship? Is it an emotional crisis? Is some external obstacle thrown into the widow or widower's path that provokes a personal crisis in him or her?

If there are children, what do they think of mom or dad dating again?

How does the widow/widower ultimately make peace with the memory of the deceased spouse to allow himself or herself to enter into another relationship and allow himself or herself to be happy again?

What does the new happily ever after for the widow/widower and their new lover look like?

How much or how little a part of their lives is the memory of the deceased spouse? What does that look like?

TROPE TRAPS

Not fleshing out the widow/widower's past relationship adequately.

Creating a clichéd bad guy or saint as the former spouse of the widow/widower.

Forcing the love interest to practically be a saint in order to wait out the never-ending emotional angst of the widow/widower.

Not showing the grief of the widow/widower or how it interferes with this new relationship.

My dead spouse said it was okay for me to date again, therefore it's all good and I have no guilt. (That's not how that usually works, as it turns out. Guilt is still had.)

The widow /widower constantly comparing the love interest to the former spouse.

Creating family and friends that are utter villains or utter saints about the widow/widower moving on with a new relationship. These people, too, will take an emotional journey over the course of this romance unfolding.

Creating children of the widow/widower who are utter monsters or utter saints.

Making the reason the widow/widower backs out of going through with the relationship trite, clichéd, or just stupid.

Giving the lover interest a savior complex. Marrying someone to save them from their grief isn't a great foundation for a long-term, healthy relationship.

Creating a completely joyless widow/widower.

Creating a completely insensitive and unfeeling widow/widower or love interest.

Short-changing the emotional journey both main characters must take for this relationship to work.

WIDOWED HERO/HEROINE TROPE IN ACTION
Movies:

- *Yours, Mine, and Ours*
- *Random Hearts*
- *Same Time Next Week*
- *Our Souls At Night*
- *October Kiss*
- *Rebecca*

- *Elsa and Fred*
- *The American President*
- *Dan in Real Life*

Books:

- *When He Was Wicked* by Julia Quinn
- *Strength From Loyalty* by Autumn Jones Lake
- *Slightly Dangerous* by Mary Balogh
- *Morning Glory* by LaVyrle Spencer
- *Virgin River* by Robyn Carr
- *Seduction* by Amanda Quick
- *The Next Always* by Nora Roberts
- *True Love and Other Disasters* by Rachel Gibson
- *The Gamble* by Kristen Ashley
- *What I Did For A Duke* by Julie Anne Long
- *The Highlander* by Kerrigan Byrne
- In Bed With A Highlander by Maya Banks
- *Vow of Deception* by Rina Kent
- *It Happened One Summer* by Tessa Bailey
- *Major Pettigrew's Last Stand* by Helen Simonson
- *The Raven Prince* by Elizabeth Hoyt

36

APPENDIX A – UNIVERSAL ROMANCE TROPES LISTED BY VOLUME

Volume 1, THE TROPOHOLIC'S GUIDE TO INTERNAL ROMANCE TROPES

- Accidental Pregnancy
- Amnesia
- Anti-Hero
- Bad Boy/Girl Reformed
- Beauty-and-the-Beast
- Burdened by Beauty/Talent
- Celibate Hero
- Clumsy/Thoughtless/Bumbling Hero/Heroine
- Cold/Serious/Uptight Hero/Heroine
- Commitment Phobia
- Damaged Hero/Heroine
- Dangerous Secret
- Disabled Hero/Heroine
- Fear of Intimacy
- Fresh Start/Do-Over
- Goody Two Shoes
- Hero/Heroine in Disguise

- Makeover
- Nerdy/Geek/Genius
- Newcomer/Outsider/Stranger
- Oblivious to Love/Last to Know
- Only One Not Married
- Plain Jane/John
- Plus Size Love
- Rebellious Hero/Heroine
- Reclusive Hero/Heroine
- Shy Hero/Heroine
- Single Parent
- Socially Awkward Hero/Heroine
- Transformation/Fixer Upper
- Ugly Duckling
- Virgin Hero/Heroine
- Widowed Hero/Heroine

Volume 2, THE TROPOHOLIC'S GUIDE TO EXTERNAL ROMANCE TROPES

- Across the Tracks/Wrong Side of the Tracks
- Best Friend's Sibling/Sibling's Best Friend
- Best Friend's/Sibling's Ex
- Best Friend's Widow/Widower
- Childhood Sweethearts/Friends
- Couples Therapy
- Cross-Cultural/Interethnic/Interracial
- Divided Loyalties
- Everyone Else Can See It
- Evil/Dysfunctional Family
- Feuding Families
- Fish Out of Water/Cowboy in the City

- Following Your Heart
- Forbidden Love
- Friends to Lovers
- Girl/Boy Next Door
- Hero/Heroine in Hiding
- Hidden/Secret Wealth
- Home for the Holiday/Vacation Fling
- Long Distance Romance
- Love Triangle
- Marriage Pact/Bargain Comes Due
- Marriage of Convenience/Fake Marriage
- No One Thinks It Will Work
- Nursing Back to Health
- On the Run/Chase
- Quest/ Search for MacGuffin
- Rags to Riches/Cinderella
- Rescue Romance/Damsel or Dude in distress
- Riches to Rags
- Rivals/Work Enemies
- Secret Baby
- Secret Identity
- Secret Organization/Secret World
- Twins Switch Places/Lookalikes

Volume 3, THE TROPOHOLIC'S GUIDE TO BACKSTORY ROMANCE TROPES

- Back From the Dead
- Billionaire
- Burned By Love/Sworn Off Love
- Bully Turned Nice Guy
- Chosen One

- Enemies to Lovers
- Engaged to/Marrying Someone Else
- Estranged Spouses/On the Rocks
- Family Skeletons
- Finding a Home
- First Love
- Forgiveness
- Guardian
- Hero/Heroine is Ex-Con
- Insta-Family
- In Love With the Wrong Person
- Is the Baby Mine
- Left At the Altar/Jilted
- Lone Wolf Tamed
- Mafia Romance
- Not Good Enough for Him/Her
- Rebound Romance
- Reconciliation/Second Chance
- Recovery/Rehabilitation
- Redemption
- Reunion
- Revenge
- Rivals
- Ruined/Ruined Reputation
- Runaway Brides
- Scandalous Hero/Heroine
- Separated/Marriage in Trouble
- Spinster/Bluestocking/On the Shelf
- Step Siblings/Stepparent
- Survivor Guilt
- Teenage Crush
- Tomboy Reformed

Volume 4, THE TROPOHOLIC'S GUIDE TO HOOK ROMANCE TROPES

- Arranged Marriage
- Baby On the Doorstep
- Boss-Employee
- Bodyguard
- Coming Home
- Deathbed Confession
- Disguised as a Male
- Drunk/Vegas Wedding
- Fake Fiancé(e)/Boyfriend/Girlfriend
- False Identity
- Fated Mates/Soul Mates
- Fling/One Night Stand
- Grumpy/Sunshine
- Innocent Cohabitation
- Love At First Sight
- Love-Hate Relationship
- Matchmaker/Matchmaker Gone Wrong
- May-December Romance
- Mistaken Identity
- Nanny/Teacher & Single Parent
- Online Love/Pen Pals
- Opposites Attract
- Pretend/Celibate Marriages
- Raising a Child Together
- Right Under Your Nose
- Road Trip/Adventure
- Running Away From Home
- Secret Crush/Secret Admirer
- Stop the Wedding
- Straight Arrow Seduced
- Stranded/Marooned/ Forced Proximity

- Terms of the Will
- Treasure Hunt
- Tricked into Marriage
- Unconsummated Marriage
- Unrequited Love

ALSO BY CINDY DEES

ABOUT THE AUTHOR

New York Times and USA Today bestselling author of over a hundred books, Cindy Dees has sold over two million books worldwide. She writes in a variety of genres, including thrillers, military adventure, romantic suspense, fantasy, and alternate history.

Cindy is the creator and executive producer of an upcoming Netflix television series based on her Helen Warwick thriller novel series about a woman assassin, and Cindy has multiple additional television and film projects in development.

A two-time RITA winner and five-time RITA finalist, she is also a two-time Holt Medallion winner, two-time winner of Romantic Times' Romantic Suspense of the Year Award and a Career Lifetime Achievement Award nominee from Romantic Times.

Cindy taught novel writing courses for seven years at a major university and has taught dozens of workshops on every aspect of writing, screenwriting, and the publishing and TV/film industries.

A former U.S. Air Force pilot and part-time spy, she draws upon real-life experience to fuel her stories of life (and sometimes love) on the edge of danger. Her social media links are at www.cindydees.com and www.cynthiadees.com.

For more information on:

- Cindy's upcoming books on genre tropes (including cozy mystery, noir mystery, thrillers, sci fi, fantasy, horror, action-adventure, and various genres of romance)
- deep dives into individual tropes
- analysis of popular movie, book, and TV show tropes
- and much, much more

you can visit www.cindydees.com/tropes to sign up for her Tropoholic's newsletter.

Made in United States
Troutdale, OR
05/05/2024

19669327R00179